Am I Fat?

Am I Fat?

Helping Young Children Accept Differences in Body Size

Joanne Ikeda, MA, RD
Priscilla Naworski, MS, CHES

Suggestions for teachers, parents and other care providers of children to age 10

ETR ASSOCIATES
Santa Cruz, California
1992

ETR Associates (Education, Training and Research) is a nonprofit organization committed to fostering the health, well-being and cultural diversity of individuals, families, schools and communities. The publishing program of ETR Associates provides books and materials that empower young people and adults with the skills to make positive health choices. We invite health professionals to learn more about our high-quality resources and our training and research programs by contacting us at P.O. Box 1830, Santa Cruz, CA 95061-1830.

10 9 8 7 6 5 4

Printed in the United States of America

Cover illustration by Marcia Quackenbush
Design by Julia Chiapella and Ann Smiley

Library of Congress Cataloging-in-Publication Data

Ikeda, Joanne P.
    Am I fat? : helping young children accept differences in body
size : suggestions for teachers, parents, and other care providers
of children to age 10 / Joanne Ikeda, Priscilla Naworski.
        p.   cm.
    Includes bibliographical references.
    ISBN 1-56071-080-2
    1. Body image in children. 2. Obesity in children—psychological
aspects. 3. Child rearing. I. Naworski, Priscilla. II. Title.
BF723.B6I54   1992
649'.7—dc20   92-19011

Title No. 569

Contents

Acknowledgments

My thanks to:

Alice Ansfield, the publisher of *Radiance* magazine, for helping me value size diversity;

Jane Kaplan, psychologist, for teaching me that "all bodies are good bodies";

Debbie Burgard, psychologist, for sharing her thoughts on what a book like this should include;

Etta Martin, social worker, for her pertinent comments on the initial outline for this book;

and my husband, Roy, and my two teenage daughters, Mindi and Jenny, who don't always find it easy to be related to someone who cares about what they eat!

—JI

Very sincere thanks are due to our editors, Kathleen Middleton and Netha Thacker. They contributed patience, skill and understanding to our process of developing this book. Their input and knowledge of health content were indispensable. A thank you in advance to all teachers and school personnel who strive to help children appreciate diversity in body size; and a special thank you to my husband, Joe, and my children, Sandra, Nancy and Matt, who encouraged me to do this project.

—PN

Preface

"The early childhood and primary education setting is an ideal place to teach children about the diversity of the world we live in. These early years, when children are developing their social skills, [are] the best time to plant the seeds of acceptance of and respect for others. Here we can teach about differences from a positive point of view. Differences can be presented as qualities that make us unique and special" (Matiella, 1991).

This book was written to help teachers, parents and other caregivers of young children provide support for diversity in body size—an area that's all too often overlooked in an American society obsessed with thinness. It offers ideas for supporting children whose body size differs from the perceived norm, as well as ways to encourage acceptance by others—both at home and at school.

In our modern American culture, children (and adults) who are larger than the perceived cultural norm may have a very difficult time. High-powered media advertising encourages Americans to consume foods that are high in fat and calories. At the same time, the media delivers a message that "thin is in" and large is unacceptable. Such messages can lead to feelings of low self-esteem and poor body image.

Teachers, parents and other caregivers who lack understanding of the variations in growth patterns that occur during childhood may unintentionally do more harm than good. Poor role modeling and attempts to limit children's food intake are ineffective and can even be harmful in dealing with children's body size issues.

Even health professionals can have difficulty dealing with issues around body image. The traditional medical approach to treatment of obesity in both children and adults has focused on calorie restriction. But recent research indicates that physical inactivity, not calorie intake, is a major factor in childhood obesity (and perhaps adult obesity, as well).

We must also acknowledge that there is a wide variation in normal size, both height and weight. This book helps adults look at their acceptance of this body size diversity and the messages about body image that they are sending to children. It encourages caring adults to look at the messages in the environment, their own feelings about the issue and the models they provide for the children in their care.

The book offers information and ideas to support teachers, parents and other caregivers in their efforts to help children accept and like their bodies. It includes specific tips on dealing with body image issues and suggestions for role modeling healthy attitudes about body size. It also offers suggestions for healthy eating, increasing physical activity for both children and adults and creating a bias-free environment in the school.

Body image and self-esteem are intimately connected. This book promotes self-esteem by promoting acceptance of diversity and empowering children to make healthy food choices. Certain areas are beyond the scope of this book, however, including deep psychological issues. Children with eating disorders or other severe body-image problems may need professional help.

In our multicultural society, Americans are learning to accept and celebrate differences. This book was written to promote the same positive attitude toward diversity in body size.

Chapter 1

Body Image—What's It All About?

As the United States becomes an increasingly multicultural society, more and more attention is given to issues of cultural and ethnic diversity and combating discrimination and prejudice. We are beginning to see the importance of teaching children to accept, respect and value differences. However, body size is one area in which diversity has not yet received widespread acceptance. Prejudice and discrimination against "fat" people may be one of the last acceptable prejudices.

Thinness has become synonymous with beauty, and fatness with ugliness. American society seems to be obsessed with body size. A recent *Glamour Magazine* survey of 33,000 women readers found that 75 percent of them felt they were too fat, even though only 25 percent were overweight and 30 percent were actually underweight. It seems likely that most women go through life feeling too fat, even though they are not.

The pressures are sometimes less obvious for men and boys, but they do exist. The "ideal" male is tall, with an athletic body, well-defined muscles and no visible fat.

"Fear of fat" has become epidemic among both adults and children in our society. By the time they are six years old, most children think that being fat is "bad." When asked to describe fat children, six year olds will use negative adjectives such as lazy, sloppy, dirty and stupid.

Specialists who treat eating disorders report seeing children as young as six who are obsessed with dieting and weight. A study of 318 middle-class girls and boys, ages eight to thirteen years old, found that 45 percent of the children wanted to be thinner. Thirty-seven percent of them had already tried to lose weight by exercising or restricting calories. Sixty-nine percent of these children reported that their mothers had been on a diet at least once.

In another study of 500 girls, ages nine to eleven, 50 percent of the nine year olds and 80 percent of the ten and eleven year olds said they were dieting to lose weight. Studies also show that 50 percent of teenage girls think they are too fat, when in fact, 83 percent of them are normal weight for their height.

This fear of fat motivates young people to take drastic steps to avoid obesity. Some preadolescents, afraid of becoming fat, restrict their calorie intake to the point that they stunt their growth and delay the onset of puberty. Some teenage boys resort to steroid use and body building in efforts to achieve the masculine "ideal."

Other teenagers, especially girls, become so desperate to lose or control their weight that they resort to self-induced vomiting or laxative abuse. Eating disorders, which were rare prior to the 1960s, are now all too common among teenage girls and may be under-reported among teenage boys. Some experts suspect that adolescent eating disorders may derive from attitudes that develop when children are much younger. Our society's preoccupation with weight clearly has a direct and detrimental effect on many young people's body image.

How Body Image Develops

Body image develops based on interactions with the people and the world around us. Newborn infants view themselves as an extension of the mother. They do not make a distinction between their bodies and the world. They trust their mothers to take care of their needs, and mothers earn this trust by consistently responding to their infants' needs in a nurturing way.

As infants develop, they begin to sense that there is a boundary between their bodies and the rest of the world. They begin to be able to tell the difference between their bodies and other objects. They also realize that their bodies are separate from the bodies of other people. At this stage, they become preoccupied with touching and tasting as they explore this new world.

During toddlerhood, the boundary between the self and others becomes more distinct. With a higher level of self-awareness, children become aware of their independence. Toddlers are eager to explore this new state of self-awareness. They often use the word "no" to assert their newly discovered autonomy.

Parents and other caregivers can foster toddlers' newfound sense of separateness by letting them do things for themselves, such as feed themselves or walk rather than be restrained in a carriage. Often a toddler will run from parents, suddenly stop, look back, and then run back. Such an episode illustrates the toddler's mixed emotions about newfound independence.

Toddlers are curious about everything and are constantly on the move. They need clear limits for acceptable behavior, because they have no judgment, little self-control and boundless energy.

Body image becomes more refined as children learn to enjoy using their bodies in recreational activities. Children are eager to climb structures, ride tricycles, run races and play catch. Adults often feel torn between fostering independence and protecting children from possible harm. At this stage, adults must set limits, while recognizing children's need to develop physical skills.

As children grow and develop, they are subject to influences beyond the primary caregivers in their lives. These social influences on body image continue throughout life. In the United States, the media is one of the most pervasive social influences.

Mass Media and Business: Profitable Cooperation

Mass media, in cooperation with business, sells the "perfect" body to us on a regular basis. Use this kind of mouthwash, drink this beverage, eat this cereal, read this diet book, buy this piece of exercise equipment, send for these pills, sign up for this diet program…and you too can have an ideal body. Americans spent

$32 billion in 1990 for weight control products and services to help us attain our dream bodies.

At any one time, 65 million Americans are dieting and will need to keep dieting in pursuit of the unattainable. For indeed, even if they manage to become thinner, the ideal will probably become thinner still. Comparing the heights, weights and body measurements of Miss America winners and *Playboy* centerfolds over the past twenty years indicates that the winners and centerfolds have become more slender every year.

How does this selling of the "perfect body" affect our children? To begin with, it promotes unrealistic expectations about the ability to attain this ideal. Children come to believe that they can have a certain body size and shape if they just buy or do the "right" things.

This pervasive image ignores the basic reality that human beings come in a wide variety of sizes and shapes, and fails to recognize that this diversity is a positive characteristic of human beings. It perpetuates a society that ostracizes and stigmatizes people who deviate too greatly from this perceived ideal.

Children come to believe that fat children and adults have made the wrong decisions and thus deserve to be treated as outcasts or inferior beings. Sadly enough, many adults feel the same way.

The Self-Esteem Connection

If someone asked you to describe your body, how would you respond? You might begin by objectively stating the facts. "I am

5 feet, 2 inches tall. I weigh 125 pounds. I have dark brown hair that is cut short."

At some point, you would reveal some of your feelings about your body. "I am not well coordinated, and as a result, I'm terrible at team sports." Eventually you would describe how others tend to view you. "People say I'm cute. I get lots of compliments on my looks, especially when I get all dressed up for a special occasion."

Body image is multidimensional. It includes the way we view ourselves as well as the way that we believe others view us. Body image is not static; it changes in response to changing feedback from the environment. Some experts suggest that body image should actually be called body images or body experience.

Self-esteem and body image are intimately connected. Body image encompasses what we think of our physical bodies, while self-esteem includes our feelings about our own worth as individuals. Body image and self-esteem are woven together to form the fabric of how we feel about ourselves, making it difficult to separate the two. People with high self-esteem usually feel positive about their bodies, while people with low self-esteem are frequently quite dissatisfied with their bodies.

Likewise, feeling good about our bodies—our appearance and capabilities—enhances self-esteem. Feelings of unhappiness or displeasure with our bodies have a negative effect on our self-esteem. To reject the appearance or capabilities of our body is to reject an integral component of our self-esteem.

Necessary Conditions of Self-Esteem

Reynold Bean (1992) has identified four conditions that are necessary to maintain a high level of self-esteem—a sense of connectiveness, a sense of uniqueness, a sense of power and a sense of models.* These four conditions refer to feelings children have about themselves and the world around them.

Children with high self-esteem experience these conditions frequently, in a variety of situations. Children with low self-esteem have difficulty feeling one or more of these conditions. Let's consider what's involved in each of these conditions and how they relate to body image.

A Sense of Connectiveness

Children with a high sense of connectiveness are able to gain satisfaction from the people, places or things they feel connected to. A strong sense of connectiveness allows children to feel secure and supported and to respect others and themselves.

The sense of connectiveness is weakened by experiences of discrimination and feelings of being different. If children are unhappy or uncomfortable with their body images, their sense of connectiveness may suffer.

---

* For a complete discussion of the four conditions model of self-esteem, see *The Four Conditions of Self-Esteem: A New Approach for Elementary and Middle Schools* by Reynold Bean, Santa Cruz, CA: ETR Associates, 1992.

A Sense of Uniqueness

Children with a high sense of uniqueness acknowledge and respect the qualities and characteristics they have that make them special and different. Confirmation from other people that these qualities and characteristics are important and good also contributes to the sense of uniqueness. A strong sense of uniqueness allows children to express and respect their own individuality and to enjoy feeling different and unusual.

Children whose body image does not fit the societal norm may feel unique in a negative way. Rather than being affirmed for what they are, they frequently feel judged for what they are not. If they feel that their individual qualities are not valuable or special, their sense of uniqueness suffers.

A Sense of Power

Children's sense of power is related to their belief in their own competence and in their ability to influence the circumstances of their lives. A strong sense of power enables children to take charge of important things in their lives, to make choices and to make desired changes.

Children who are perceived to be larger than normal may be criticized by others for their behavior around food and physical activity. Especially if those who care for them try to limit their food intake, these children may begin to feel that they are incapable of controlling their eating. Children who don't feel confidence in their bodies may not feel able to direct the body's performance in physical activity. Such experiences have a negative effect on a child's sense of power.

A Sense of Models

Children need standards and values to help them make sense of the world. Human models are real or fictional people whose characteristics and actions we admire and seek to emulate. Philosophical models are the ideas, beliefs and values promoted by society, religion, families, etc., that guide our actions and choices. Finally, operational models are the automatic, almost subconscious responses and behaviors that develop as a result of constant, repetitive experience (saying please and thank you, standing up when one is introduced, etc.).

All these types of models are reference points that guide behavior. These reference points help children set their own goals, values, personal standards and ideals.

In our weight-conscious society, children, especially larger children, may have a difficult time finding models. Children from varied cultural and ethnic backgrounds and children with other physical differences may see few models to emulate in popular American culture. The lack of models emphasizes children's differences in an unaffirming way.

Parents, teachers and other caregivers are children's most important human models. When we model respect for and acceptance of ourselves and others, regardless of body size or other physical attributes, we send a powerful message to our children that helps build their self-esteem.

Being Sensitive to Body Image Issues

Children learn what is important to adults by listening to them and by watching them. When they hear adults expressing dissatisfaction with their bodies, they begin to believe that being an adult means being dissatisfied with one's body. And when they hear adults disparaging the bodies of others, they mimic this behavior by teasing other children about their bodies.

Adults must ask themselves, what kind of a role model am I for children with respect to body image? Have I inadvertently promoted fear of fat in children by my words and actions? Questions to ponder include:

- Am I dissatisfied with my body size and shape?

- Do I talk about my unhappiness with my body? Whom do I talk to, and who might overhear what I have to say?

- Am I always on a diet or going on a diet? Who knows when I'm on a diet and how do they know?

- Do I express guilt when I eat certain foods, or do I refuse to eat certain foods while commenting that I am dieting to lose weight?

- Do I make negative comments about other people's sizes and shapes? Do I feel superior to them because I think my body is better than theirs?

- Am I prejudiced against overweight children and adults? Do I avoid making friends with overweight people? Am I embarrassed to be seen in public with overweight people?

🕊️ As a teacher, do I tend to pay less attention to overweight children in my classroom? Have I ever been surprised when such a child, who I thought was not very bright, got a high grade on a standardized test? Has a parent ever complained that I was treating an overweight child unfairly in some way?

These soul-searching questions have no right or wrong answers, but exploring your responses to them can lead to personal resolutions for change and self-improvement, as well as offer opportunities to educate children. Here are some possible actions you can take:

🕊️ Adhere to a philosophy that it is not fair to judge others on the basis of body size, shape, color or other physical attributes. Use this philosophy to shape your own behavior.

🕊️ Call a halt to self-flagellation over alleged failures to achieve the ideal body. Recognize that the pursuit of thinness reflects a superficial value system.

🕊️ Write complimentary letters to companies that sponsor television programming that positively represents diversity in appearance. Share these letters with children, and explain why you have written them.

🕊️ Buy products from companies that make realistic claims in advertising or on labels. Point out unrealistic claims to children, and help them understand that the purpose of advertising is to sell products.

We need to look carefully at the American cultural ideal that glorifies thinness and acknowledge that this ideal is not a universal standard. Even in the United States, various body shapes have been in and out of fashion over the years. For example, as recently as the 1950s, the ideal American woman was much more voluptuous than the current ideal.

We also need to be sensitive to body image issues other than weight, including height and physical abilities. As we strive to foster healthy body images in children, we should be consistent in promoting the following concepts:

- Human beings come in a wide variety of sizes and shapes and have different physical characteristics and abilities. This diversity should be accepted, respected and valued.

- We respect the bodies of others even when they are quite different from our own bodies.

- Everyone's body is a good body.

Chapter 2

Diversity Is Normal

Children, and adults, come in a wide variety of sizes, shapes and abilities. This diversity of body sizes and shapes is affected by both biological and cultural factors. Understanding this diversity helps us respect and value it. When we understand and accept this diversity, we reduce feelings of frustration and worry for children who are at either end of the spectrum.

Differential Growth Rates: A Fact of Life

Children grow at very different rates. They grow rapidly in the first year of life, and weight usually doubles in the first six months. By fourteen months, most infants have tripled their birth weight. Growth then slows down and becomes more gradual.

Just before puberty, children experience a second rapid growth spurt. This spurt usually begins at about eight to ten years of age for girls and at about eleven to thirteen years for boys. Growth is not as rapid as in infancy, but it is still an amazing thing to witness.

Growth in height and weight do *not* happen simultaneously. Children may start to look chubby or chunky because they have put on weight in the last few months but have not grown taller. After a sudden growth spurt in height, children will appear slender. Some children may look like string beans because they have grown taller but not heavier. Weight usually catches up eventually.

Even different parts of the body grow at different rates. Foot size is a good example. A child may go through two or three shoe sizes within a matter of months.

The moral of all of this is to be patient. A child who appears to be chubby may grow into her or his weight. A tall, skinny child may "fill out" in a matter of months. Health care professionals can help adults assess children's growth. If a professional concludes that growth in height cannot possibly take care of a weight problem, he or she will recommend a course of action.

Any approach to children's weight issues should be designed in ways that will nurture self-esteem and promote a positive body image. Understanding some of the biological and cultural factors that determine or affect body size can help us accept differences and diversity.

The Role of Heredity:
The Nature-Versus-Nurture Debate

Every human being begins as an embryo, created when an egg is penetrated by a sperm. The embryo receives 23 chromosomes from each parent, for a total of 46 chromosomes.

Chromosomes are rod-shaped bodies found in the nucleus of human cells. Each chromosome carries approximately 20,000 genes. Genes are the biologic units of heredity that contain patterns for making all body proteins. These patterns compose the DNA (deoxyribonucleic acid) found in the nucleus of the cell. These patterns will be used over and over again throughout a person's lifetime to create new body proteins, and these patterns determine many things about a person's physical characteristics.

The following physical characteristics are determined entirely by a person's genes:

- sex
- eye color
- hair color
- curliness of hair
- skin color
- blood type
- hereditary diseases, such as cystic fibrosis, Down's syndrome, hemophilia, muscular dystrophy, phenylketonuria (PKU), sickle cell anemia, Tay-Sachs syndrome, Turner's syndrome

We can alter some of these characteristics. For example, we can put on colored contact lenses to change eye color, or have a permanent to curl hair. However, these are temporary changes that are produced artificially. We cannot permanently change eye color, hair color or the curliness of the hair. These things are determined before birth by our genes.

Environment is a broad term that includes such diverse things as the following:

- premature birth
- oxygen deprivation during or after birth
- nutrition from conception throughout life
- exposure to drugs, tobacco, alcohol or radiation
- exposure to disease, either viral or bacterial in nature
- emotional state
- behavioral interactions with caregivers (parents, extended family members, babysitters), siblings, teachers and peers
- socioeconomic class
- culture and/or ethnicity

The following human characteristics are the result of the interaction of heredity with the environment:

- predisposition to certain diseases, such as alcoholism, heart disease, cancer, diabetes, hypertension, schizophrenia, depression and obesity
- personality characteristics of being introverted or extroverted
- intelligence
- height
- weight

Note that both height and weight are the result of the interaction of genetics and environment. For many years, experts thought that genetics played a minimal role in the development of obesity. However, recent studies have led scientists to conclude that the role of genetics is much more pronounced than was originally thought.

Scientists are not in agreement as to how significant the role of genetics is. But a great deal of research is going on in this area, and new developments will probably enable scientists to better quantify the role that both genetics and environment play.

There is no doubt that obesity tends to run in families. A child with no obese parent has only a 3 to 7 percent risk of becoming obese. This risk increases to 40 percent if one parent is obese and to 80 percent if both parents are obese.

Obese parents may have food and activity habits that foster their obesity. Children of obese parents may acquire such habits from their parents. Of course, the biological offspring of obese parents also have the parents' genes, so the tendency to obesity could be genetic.

The weights of adoptive children are highly correlated with the weights of their biological parents and are not correlated with the weights of their adoptive parents. This finding supports the conclusion that genetics does indeed play a significant role in body weight as well as body height.

A frank discussion with children about heredity and the difference between things we can change and things we can't may be especially helpful for children who have concerns about body size. Adults can encourage children to accept body characteristics that can't be changed by modeling such acceptance of their own bodies. Adults can also model making healthy choices to change the characteristics that we can control.

Cultural Influences: A World of Difference

Weight is also influenced by cultural beliefs and practices. Other societies have views of weight that are very different from those embraced by American society. Many Americans believe that being fat is unhealthy and undesirable, while many people from other cultures believe the opposite. In some cultures, overweight is highly prized and valued.

For example, only the rich have enough food to become fat in a country where resources are scarce. In such countries, having a wife and children who are fat is considered visible proof that a man is a good provider and takes good care of his family. It means that he has a job and earns money that is used to buy food or that he is a successful farmer who can afford to consume his crops and livestock. Being able to eat well may be a sign of social status, proof that a family is doing well financially.

In some cultures, parents are proud of their chubby children. They may encourage children to overeat because being fat has health advantages in poorer communities. Carrying extra weight can help a child or adult live through times of famine and can help infants and toddlers live through infections that might otherwise kill because there is no access to antibiotics.

In light of this, it is not surprising that new immigrants to the United States are confused by advice about feeding their children less food or less of certain kinds of food. They may never have heard of "junk food," because processed, high-fat snack foods with low nutrient density were not easily available in their homelands.

When they settle in the United States, they are suddenly bombarded by advertisements proclaiming that soft drinks, potato chips, snack crackers, cakes, cookies and anything that comes from a fast food restaurant are desirable American foods. Obviously, the popular media does not present the basics of a balanced diet or a realistic picture of the "ideal" body.

In some cultures, the ideal body image is much heavier than the American mainstream cultural ideal. The challenge is to teach immigrants how to select a balanced diet in their new land and help them understand that in this country obesity may have health risks, just as being underweight did in their homeland, without encouraging them to adopt the American obsession with thinness or the idea that there is an ideal body size and shape that everyone should strive to attain.

☙ ☙ ☙

New research in the area of body size continues to provide information about the interconnections between heredity, environment and weight, as well as the physiological processes involved in weight gain and loss. As we promote acceptance of body size diversity, we can encourage and model healthy behaviors, including eating healthy food and being physically active. Such actions promote good health for all children, regardless of body size.

Chapter 3

Nutrition and Physical Activity

As children grow and mature, they gradually assume increasing responsibility for practicing good health habits. These habits include eating a variety of nutritious foods, being physically active and getting enough rest.

Children need simple, accurate explanations of the importance of practicing healthy habits. Children are more apt to adopt healthy habits if they understand how these habits contribute to health and if they see their parents and teachers modeling them. Habits that promote and contribute to a positive body image are particularly important to instill given the pressures children face from the media and society in regard to body image.

As a society, Americans have become so weight-conscious that those who treat eating disorders have seen children as young as five years old who are preoccupied with dieting. Recent medical research indicates, however, that dieting is not a very effective way to control weight and may actually have harmful effects. And low-calorie diets are seldom recommended for children, as they can endanger normal growth.

Children who are concerned about their body size should be assured that they are lovable and capable just as they are. They need to understand that people come in small, medium and large sizes and that their own bodies will change as they grow. Children must be taught that their growing bodies need healthy food and exercise.

When children learn to accept and respect the diversity of human appearance, they are better able to love their bodies for what they are and to choose to take good care of them. When health rather than thinness is made the goal, everyone's body can attain its own ideal condition.

Trusting the Body

Children need to learn that they can trust their bodies to let them know when they are hungry and when they are full. Infants eat in response to body hunger cues and cease eating in response to feelings of satiety (a feeling of fullness and satisfaction). As we get older, however, external cues may confuse our natural ability to regulate our food intake.

During the preschool years, children may learn to eat in response to environmental cues rather than in response to body hunger cues. For example, some children get so used to eating while they are watching television that watching television becomes a signal to eat.

Adults who try to control the amount of food children eat are inadvertently sending the message that children cannot trust their bodies to tell them when they are hungry and when they are full and that someone else has to do this for them. But if children are to accept responsibility for good eating habits, they must believe that they can handle this responsibility and, indeed, nutrition research shows that they can.

Adults may find it difficult to let children who are overweight eat as much as they want. Sometimes health professionals or relatives will pressure parents to restrict children's food intake, or adults may think they are helping children by preventing them from eating too much.

However, attempting to control the amount of food children eat invariably backfires. Children worry that they won't get enough food to satisfy their hunger and may begin to sneak food, hide food, beg food from friends or buy food when adults aren't around. Such children end up eating more food rather than less.

Larger children may need assurance that their body signals can help them regulate their food intake. You can explain to these children, "Your body tells you when you're hungry, and that is when you should eat. You can also trust your body to tell you when you've had enough food, and that is when you should stop eating. Since I can't put myself inside your body, I can't tell whether you are hungry or not. And I can't tell when you have had enough to eat and are full. I am trusting you to do that for yourself."

Sometimes you will need to strike a balance between trusting children's assessment of their food needs and exerting some control in situations where children may not be able to judge those needs accurately. For example, children may be stimulated to overeat at fast food restaurants because there are so many tempting foods to choose from. They may want to order far more food than they need to satisfy hunger.

In these cases, adults can limit the quantity of food ordered but still allow children to follow their internal hunger cues by offering options such as the following:

    ⁎ You can order one milkshake to share (with a sibling or friend). If you are still thirsty after you drink that with your meal, I will buy another milkshake.

    ⁎ No, you can't order both French fries and fried onion rings, because that is too much fried food. But you can have one or the other. Which one would you like?

Explaining Good Nutrition

All children need to be encouraged to eat a variety of healthy foods. Adults who care for children can make a point of providing healthy food choices for regular meals and planned snacks.

Teachers, parents and other caregivers can help children understand what healthy food is by explaining that food has things in it called *nutrients*. Nutrients are vitamins, minerals, proteins, fats, carbohydrates and water.

Tell children that their bodies use nutrients in the following ways:

- Growth—See how big you are now compared to when you were a baby? Your body used the nutrients in food to help you grow.

- Repair—Remember when you fell down and hurt yourself? You got a cut or a bruise. Now it is all healed. Your body used the nutrients in food to heal itself.

- Running the body—Do you know that your body works 24 hours a day? Even while you are sleeping, your body is using nutrients to help digest food, to keep your heart beating, your lungs breathing, and your mind dreaming. There is a lot going on in your body all the time. The body uses nutrients from food to keep things going.

- Energy for work and play—Your body uses the nutrients in food for energy so you can walk, run, jump, play games, learn, do your homework, and so on. If you don't get enough of the energy nutrients, you'll be tired.

Teachers, parents and other caregivers can also explain that some foods have more nutrients than others, which is why we eat some foods more often and other foods less often.

Nutrient Density

The key to good nutrition is eating a wide variety of nutrient dense foods. Just what is a nutrient dense food? It is a food that has a lot of nutritional value, i.e, vitamins, minerals, protein, complex carbohydrates, in relationship to its calorie value. A food with low nutrient density will have very little nutritional value in relationship to its calorie value.

Let's compare the nutrient density of three beverages in terms of some of the nutrients they contribute to the diet.

Drink	Calcium	Riboflavin	Calories
Nonfat Milk (8 oz.)	352 mg.	.48 mg.	100
Whole Milk (8 oz.)	291 mg.	.40 mg.	150
Cola Soda (8 oz.)	7 mg.	.00 mg.	101

As you can see, nonfat milk provides the most calcium and riboflavin. It is also lowest in calories. Therefore, the nutrient density of nonfat milk is very high.

The nutrient density of whole milk is good, but not as good as nonfat milk. It has a lot of calcium and riboflavin, but it also has more calories because there is fat in it. The fat has been removed from nonfat milk.

The cola soda has the poorest nutrient density. It contributes a tiny amount of calcium and no riboflavin, yet it has a calorie value comparable to that of nonfat milk.

Within each of the basic food groups, foods can be categorized as having high nutrient density, good nutrient density or lower nutrient density. We all need to choose foods in the high nutrient density category often. Most of the foods we eat should fall in this category.

Foods from the good nutrient density category round out the day's food intake. Even though they are higher in calories, they are good sources of nutrients.

The term *junk food* is often used to describe foods with low nutrient density. Try to avoid the use of this term, because it implies a value judgment rather than a factual assessment of the nutritional quality of a food.

Foods from the lower nutrient density group should be eaten only occasionally. Don't make the mistake of making these foods completely forbidden fruit. Children who are never allowed to eat candy, ice cream, potato chips, hamburgers, French fries and such will begin to view these off-limits foods as very desirable.

Compromise by buying limited amounts of such foods—just enough so that children don't feel deprived—but don't let these foods displace more nutritious alternatives on a regular basis.

Regular Meals and Snacks

Establishing a daily routine that includes regular meals and snacks is important to children's nutritional well-being. Children who skip meals are apt to overeat at the next meal because they are very hungry. Regular meals and snacks keep children's hunger satisfied, so there is no need to overeat.

Children who are eating constantly are also apt to overeat, because they spend too much time consuming food. Constant snacking also reduces food consumption at meals, which is when foods high in nutrient density are most apt to be served. Discourage this pattern of eating, popularly known as "grazing."

School-age children are often hungry when they get home from school. After school is a good time for snacking, because it's usually two or three hours before the evening mealtime. That amount of time allows children to have a snack and still be hungry again in time for dinner.

A good family rule is, No snacking during the hour before dinner. If you feel children cannot wait an hour and really need to eat, you can serve part of the meal early. For example, let them drink half a glass of milk or eat some carrot sticks.

Another good family rule is, No snacking while watching TV. When children become used to watching TV while snacking, they may want to begin eating meals in front of the television set. The association of TV with food becomes ingrained, and then every time they turn on the TV, they feel hungry!

Mealtime Issues

Parents and other adult caregivers decide what food to serve at mealtimes and snack times. These adults are really the gatekeepers of the food supply, because they decide what foods to buy and how to prepare them.

Favorite Foods

Most parents don't mind responding to children's special requests to have a favorite item at dinner if it hasn't been served for a while. However, parents have to be careful not to become short-order cooks, or they will find themselves catering to every family member's likes and dislikes. As one mother finally responded when nagged to prepare different choices for each family member, "I am not running a restaurant!"

Catering to individual family members' food likes and dislikes also encourages children to narrow their food choices to just a favorite few, which runs counter to an important principle of nutrition. We need to eat a wide variety of foods to get all of the nutrients we need for good health. Children (and adults) should eat lots of different foods.

Sometimes children may want to overeat their favorite foods. For example, a child whose favorite dessert is sweet potato pie might want to eat half of a pie. You can explain to the child that there are other family members who also want their share of the pie and make a rule that everyone must have a share before anyone gets seconds. You can also offer children seconds of other foods available, preferably nutrient dense ones, instead of the particular favorite.

What About Vegetables?

Many children are not fond of vegetables. "Do I have to eat these?" is a common response when something green appears on the plate. Should adults let children eat everything but the vegetables at mealtimes? Or should they insist that children eat their vegetables?

One way to handle this dilemma is to have a rule about the "delicious minimum." If children don't like a food on their plates, they only have to eat the "delicious minimum" of that food. Adults can decide how much the delicious minimum is going to be, perhaps two tablespoons. If the rule is clear and consistently enforced, struggles over disliked foods should be greatly reduced. Children who know they only have to consume the delicious minimum will offer fewer protests.

Many children reject foods that they have never eaten before or even familiar foods prepared in a new way. Research has shown that children are more apt to eat foods that they have at least tasted before. The "delicious minimum" ensures that children at least taste what is being served. When we can get children to taste these foods, we increase the chance that more of this food will be eaten the next time it is served.

The "delicious minimum" also appeals to the strong sense of fair play that is so prevalent among elementary school youngsters. Children usually recognize the fairness of the delicious minimum rule.

Another way to increase vegetable consumption is to serve vegetables raw instead of cooked. Many children don't like the strong flavors that cooking brings out in vegetables. They find the taste of fresh vegetables much more appealing.

Carrot sticks, broccoli trees, cucumber rounds, tomato wedges, celery poles, cauliflower chunks, green pepper strips—choose two or three of these vegetables and arrange them attractively on a bit of romaine lettuce, butter lettuce or fresh spinach leaves. Serve with a dressing made by mixing a packaged dry dressing with plain low-fat yogurt.

Foods a Child Hates

Everyone, including children, should be allowed to have one or two foods that they never have to eat. Of course, it's important not to let this list get too long. It should not become a list of all the foods that children would rather not eat. Instead, it should be a short list of foods that the child really dislikes. For unknown or previously untried foods, the delicious minimum rule should apply.

Physical Activity and Body Image

Physical activity is critical to fitness and health and also has an important impact on body image. Children who think their bodies are too large or too small or too clumsy often feel uncomfortable about participating in physical activity. On the other hand, learning to enjoy physical activity can encourage appreciation of and respect for one's body.

Parents, teachers and other caregivers need to have realistic expectations with respect to children's physical skills and to patiently support development and refinement of those skills. Children who receive positive feedback from caring adults will view their bodies in positive ways.

Tell children what they are doing right, not wrong. "Bend your arm a little more, John...there, that's good!" is much more likely to foster a positive body image than the statement, "You're holding your arm too stiff, which is why you keep missing the ball." Constructive feedback helps children feel that they can master skills, while criticism tends to foster a sense of hopelessness and helplessness.

We can help ensure that children enjoy physical activity by offering noncompetitive activities at their level of fitness. We can help children develop their fitness and abilities by allowing them to set their own goals and by offering time and instruction for skill development. Appropriate physical activity will help children feel good about their bodies.

Avoiding the TV Trap

Survey after survey indicates that American children are not achieving high levels of fitness. One of the greatest contributors to this lack of fitness is television. Children who spend most of their free time watching television and playing video games simply are not going to be physically fit.

Recent research indicates that inactivity is an even bigger contribution to childhood obesity than calorie intake. The more time a child spends watching television, the greater the risk of obesity. Restricting children's television viewing and video-game playing can make a far bigger contribution to their health and well-being than restricting the food they eat.

You can check on just how much time children are watching television and playing video games by keeping a television viewing log for a week. Most parents and caregivers are shocked when they find out that their children are watching more than twenty hours of television a week on a regular basis.

It is not easy to begin limiting the amount of time children are allowed to watch TV. Adults need to be firm. Begin by stating what the rules are. For example: You can watch television or play video games for an hour and a half after school on weekdays. Then you are to turn the television set off. The television will not be turned on Monday through Thursday after dinner. This is the time when you are expected to work on your homework. Even if you finish your homework, you still are not allowed to watch television.

After the rules are stated, they need to be consistently enforced. Without consistent enforcement, children will return to their old habits.

Encouraging Physical Activity

Of course, just turning off the TV set doesn't automatically mean that children will be more physically active. Adults need to take an active role in encouraging and supporting physical activity. The best way to encourage children to be active is to actively participate with them. Here are some other suggestions:

- Emphasize fun and enjoyment rather than competition and strenuous "body building" workouts. If children don't have fun and enjoy themselves, they won't want to participate in physical activity on a regular basis.

- Look into the activities local parks and recreation departments offer for youngsters. Many such departments offer classes in dance, tennis, karate, gymnastics or other physical activity. Others organize volleyball, softball, baseball, basketball and flag football games.

- Consider finding a place for children to swim inexpensively on a regular basis. Some localities have community pools. Many YWCAs and YMCAs also have pools.

- Look into sports leagues in your neighborhood. Is there a soccer league, a baseball league, a hockey league or other sports league that your children can become actively involved in? Look for a league that emphasizes skill development and team cooperation rather than competition.

❧ If your neighborhood is safe and includes other children, encourage children to spend time outside playing kickball, badminton, hopscotch, hide and seek or other games.

❧ If you have a dog, assign a child the chore of taking the dog for a daily walk.

❧ Provide toys that encourage physical activity, such as ice skates or roller skates, hula hoops, balls, bats, baseball gloves, jump ropes, Frisbees, punch balls and kites.

❧ Engage in physical activity as a family on the weekend. Go for a hike. Walk through a zoo or museum. Run around the track at a nearby school. Ride bikes. Explore a new park you've never visited before. Swim at a lake. Volunteer to help with chores at a homeless shelter, emergency food pantry or soup kitchen, or local hospital.

❧ ❧ ❧

Eating a variety of healthy foods and engaging in regular physical activity benefit everyone, regardless of body size. When we help children learn to take care of their bodies, we promote their general health and well-being, as well as a positive body image.

Chapter 4

Body Image in the School Setting

Body image both derives from and contributes to our relationships with others, as well as individual development. Some of the factors involved in this complex interplay include:

- ❧ the attitudes, values and expectations of others
- ❧ our interactions with others (parents, caregivers, teachers, peers)
- ❧ the physical settings for these interactions

School administrators, teachers and other staff can take an active role in promoting a school environment that supports and values all children regardless of body size or ability.

Creating a Bias-Free School Environment

The school environment and culture can and should be bias free. Rules for student behavior can reflect acceptance of diversity and make it clear that respect for others is a value held by the school. Rules should be developed with input from students, teaching and support staff, and parents.

Once rules are determined, they should be clearly posted in the common area of the school and in all classrooms. Teachers and school campus supervisors should review the rules frequently with the students. All students and staff can have a hand in enforcing the rules.

An established rule should have a predetermined, fair and consistent punishment associated with breaking it. The punishment should be determined by the same group that established the rule so that all parties will agree to it.

In regard to body image issues, the following two concepts can be used as guidelines for establishing rules of behavior:

- We respect the bodies of others even when they are quite different from our own.

- Everyone's body is a good body.

In a school climate that promotes these concepts, children's views of their own and others' bodies can be affected in a positive way. They can come to feel proud of their various physical attributes and skills. They will also feel supported in developing their skills and physical abilities.

However, no matter how hard we try to establish positive, supportive environments, at some point children may encounter situations that are nonsupportive or even hostile. Such situations often take the form of teasing by other children.

Teasing and Name Calling

Larger children are often teased or called names. Put-downs that refer to a child's size may be heard in the classroom, on the playground, in the gym, in the neighborhood—anywhere children have time and an environment that permits hassling or ridiculing others who are different from the norm.

Children are very sensitive to such teasing and name calling. It is of little comfort to the larger child that the same thing happens to children who get the best grades, children who wear glasses and children of minority ethnic groups.

Teachers, parents and other caregivers who allow children to tease each other about physical traits or abilities should realize that such teasing contributes to low self-esteem and poor body image. Essentially, teachers, parents or other caregivers are condoning this behavior when they allow it to go on in their presence.

Teasing is an assertive action that is best countered by an equally assertive action. "Turning the other cheek" doesn't work and may actually invite further verbal and even physical abuse.

Children can be given stock responses to use in such situations. "Sticks and stones may break my bones, but names will never hurt me" is an old standby. A more modern version might be "I really don't care what you call me because you are not a friend of mine. If you were, you wouldn't be saying mean things like that to me."

All children can benefit from learning coping skills to help them manage the stress, disappointment and hurt they may feel when teased or ridiculed. Effective coping skills include physical activities such as walking, jogging or punching a pillow to work off frustration. With practice, children can learn to use these skills instead of ineffective strategies such as fighting or bullying or putting themselves down.

Clear and consistent rules about teasing and name calling can go a long way toward remedying such situations, as the following example shows:

> Skyview School's students, parents and staff decided that two important rules for a healthy psychological environment were that all persons at the school be treated with respect and that there would be no name calling at the school. The fair punishment decided on for breaking the rule was a five-minute time-out for the name caller, during which he or she was to reflect on the hurt that the name calling caused others.

> Children who have three or more time-outs for name calling are sent to the school principal or counselor for a conference. Students' parents are informed about the conference. Teachers and support staff remind students about this rule frequently. They also model the desired behavior by treating all students and staff with respect and using no derogatory names. Everyone at Skyview School knows that this is the acceptable way to behave at their

school, and the problems of name calling have been eliminated.

Modeling a Healthy Body Image

School staff members are important role models for their students. When staff members are preoccupied with dieting, children get a message that dieting and constant concern about weight are encouraged. If children constantly hear teachers discuss weight loss efforts with students or staff members, such efforts come to seem part of normal behavior.

Staff members should be careful to model good attitudes and not allow students to overhear conversations about weight or dieting. A conversation that starts with "You've lost some weight, haven't you?" indicates to children that a person's weight is his or her most important personal quality. Teachers should not share their dieting efforts with children or encourage children to be a support group for their efforts.

Sometimes teachers, consciously or unconsciously, display a distaste for children's body size by not calling on or recognizing larger children as often as they do the children of normal size in the classroom. Teachers need to be vigilant to keep their classroom relationships and interchanges bias free and fair to all children.

A teacher who models good health habits provides a more valuable health lesson than any textbook lesson ever written. Teachers can model habits of good diet, grooming and cleanliness, exercise, a drug-free lifestyle and stress management.

For example, if the teacher's sack lunch for the field trip has carrot sticks instead of a bag of chips, children will notice and will learn about food choices. When it is time to reward children for good work, the teacher who distributes raisins or unsalted peanuts instead of candy is teaching about healthful snack choices as well as rewarding the students.

Sometimes teachers reward their classes by providing a video to watch, but this activity models sedentary activities. Free time on the playground or a walking field trip are rewards that offer the benefits of better lifestyle training. Most children spend too much time in front of a television set, and they need to be encouraged to move more and to enjoy activity.

A school site that is committed to a comprehensive health program will provide health promotion activities for its staff. Such activities may include after-school walking clubs, aerobics classes before or after school and healthy munchies in the staff room. Students who see their teachers involved in these activities will recognize that teachers practice what they preach.

The school's site health promotion program should also provide all staff members with sources of valid health information. Reliable health newsletters or journals can be ordered for use in the staff room. Lunch-time or after-school inservice on topics such as nutrition, stress management, self-esteem and physical fitness should be provided periodically. All of these programs enable teachers to be better health models. Young children usually learn more from what they see others doing than from what they are told.

School Food Service

The school food service program provides between one third and one half of the nutritional intake for many children. Since its inception in the early 1940s, this federal program has had three goals:

- to feed hungry children
- to provide examples of nutritionally balanced meals that are of a quantity and composition appropriate for children
- to be a learning laboratory for nutrition education

A well-planned school lunch menu will contain both raw and prepared food selections that adhere to the U. S. Dietary Guidelines. The foods should be low in fat, salt and sugar and high in complex carbohydrates, i.e., fruits and vegetables, whole grains and other sources of fiber. When such well-planned meals are served to children on a daily basis, they begin to see a pattern for healthful eating and also develop a taste for these foods of high nutritional quality.

Children of all body sizes need to be encouraged to eat to satisfy normal hunger and satiety patterns. The cafeteria monitors and the food service staff should be aware of this need and should not demand that children clean their plates. Children should be able to eat when they are hungry and stop when they are full, and they should be encouraged to recognize and follow their own body signals.

Menu Modification and Planning

Well-planned menus must take into account the foods that children traditionally enjoy and accept. For example, French fries can still appear on the menu with a simple change in preparation. Oven fries are much lower in fat and still appeal to children. Substituting canned fruits packed in fruit juice rather than heavy syrup, or salad dressing made with low-fat yogurt rather than mayonnaise, can prove to children that nutritious food choices can be both tasty and healthy.

As menus are being modified and improved, the food service staff should educate children, staff and parents about the changes. Notices in the cafeteria, memos to teachers and printed menus for parents can be used to educate the food service clients.

School food service staff can participate in classrooms as part of the nutrition education team. When invited to make a classroom presentation, a food service staff member might provide the opportunity for the class to plan a menu that would be served in the lunch or breakfast program in the future.

After a presentation on the required components of the meal, the speaker can ask children to select food items that meet the requirements and are of high nutritional value. Once planned, the meal can be added to an upcoming month's menu cycle and credit can be given to the class that planned the menu. Many food service programs have found that such an activity increases student interest in the program, students' awareness of the nutritional value of the meal and even sales and participation.

Physical Education

Many adults have vivid memories of ridicule and failure in their school physical education classes. High quality school physical education classes have the potential to help all children feel good about themselves, regardless of body size or physical ability. On the other hand, poor programs can cause children to hate gym class and, consequently, hate physical activity for the rest of their lives.

One research study found that many physical education teachers think large children are less skillful at athletics and are embarrassed to be seen in gym clothing. Such attitudes have a negative impact on the self-esteem of such children and can increase their sense of failure. Teachers with such attitudes are likely to overlook or ignore the larger children in their classes. They therefore miss the opportunity to involve these children in physical activity that can offer them a feeling of success.

Physical education teachers must be well educated about the growth and development of children. They must also be able to demonstrate positive attitudes toward children of all sizes and abilities. These two components form the basis of a successful school physical education program. In such a program, children learn that fitness is possible for people of a variety of sizes and that enjoyment is as important as performance.

A child should never be blamed for a team's losing. Such blaming can occur if competitive teams are set up with children of widely different skill levels. Even the process of picking the teams can be an embarrassing and painful experience for some children. Being the last child picked for a team is a humiliation long remembered.

Adults can limit the negative impact of such situations by planning activities that do not involve team competition or by preselecting teams to make them evenly matched as to skill and development level. Encourage children to value the opportunities to participate in activity, and try to downplay the emphasis on winning. Allowing a child who is not as skilled in athletics to be team captain provides an opportunity for him or her to develop leadership qualities and be accepted by classmates.

Skilled physical education teachers can help all children find many physical activities they are good at, no matter what their development level. Plan lessons with a variety of activities, and allow adequate time and instruction to develop the special skills children need to be successful at sports.

To do this, you must have enough equipment and space available for all children to have the opportunity to practice the skills and then to participate in the activity. Many books and activity guides suggest group fitness activities that use inexpensive materials, sometimes in a confined space. (See Suggested Readings.)

All children in the physical education class should be encouraged to set personal goals. Children's success in the class can be judged by how well they attain their goals instead of predetermined criteria such as a national fitness test.

Children should be allowed to achieve their "personal best" rather than being held to a standardized test criteria for success. Praise for even small successes and skill development is especially important to children who feel inadequate and awkward because of a poor body image.

The School Nurse

The school nurse has a unique opportunity to help children feel comfortable with their bodies and to communicate their concerns to teachers and parents. All children need love and acceptance, no matter what their body size, and the school nurse, as a neutral third party, can convey this need to other adults. The school nurse is also the natural person to suggest a referral to a medical or nutritional specialist who can counsel parents and teachers if a child has a serious weight problem.

Many school health service programs routinely measure height and weight and keep growth records for students. When these measurements are taken, the nurse or nurse's assistant should be careful to do the measuring and recording in a positive, reassuring manner. All such interchanges between the nurse and children should be confidential.

If a child expresses dissatisfaction with his or her body size or weight, the nurse can provide reassuring information about expected individual variations in growth and development. Just knowing that these differences are normal can comfort children and ease their feelings of concern.

Parents, too, will often feel free to express concerns about children's size to the school nurse. The nurse should be prepared to discuss these concerns based on information from the child's height and weight chart and a thorough knowledge of normal child development patterns.

The nurse should stress that dieting is inadvisable for young children and that emphasis should be placed instead on nutritious meals and snacks, regular physical activities and providing a supportive environment.

❧ ❧ ❧

A schoolwide commitment to promoting positive body images for students and staff can have important health benefits. People who feel good about their bodies are more likely to engage in health-promoting behaviors.

Chapter 5

Body Image Issues
in the Classroom

A comprehensive school health education curriculum encompasses many areas of health instruction that can address the issue of body image directly or indirectly at all grade levels. A school that has such a comprehensive program in place will easily be able to facilitate such a curriculum focus. One that does not can begin by addressing such issues in classroom programs.

Integrating discussions around body image into other areas of the curriculum will reinforce health education lessons related to body image. When students hear a consistent message in many different content areas, the message becomes more believable and is instilled as part of the school culture. The following suggestions for classroom activities explore important ideas and themes related to body image. Feel free to adapt these activities to fit the needs of your particular students.

Classroom Activities on Accepting Diversity

You can create large or small group activities that emphasize the importance of accepting and affirming diversity in all its many forms, including body size. Such activities can also increase children's awareness of bias and prejudice.

For Children Ages Five to Seven

—ALIKE AND DIFFERENT—

Ask children to make a list of ways that people are alike. Let each child make a drawing that shows a way that people are alike. For example, all people can think and learn; all people have feelings; all people want to have friends and fun. Cluster the phrases or pictures on a bulletin board under the heading *All people are alike.*

Then ask children to think of ways that people are different. Let them make a list and drawings of the ways that people can be different. These might include different hair, different eye color, different body size, different families, different likes and dislikes and different things that they can and cannot do. Cluster the phrases or pictures on a bulletin board under the heading *All people are different.*

Ask children to discuss how these differences make people interesting. Ask them to consider each of the ways that people are different. Ask if the difference means someone is good or bad on the inside. Help children to understand that what is seen on the outside is just a small part of the real person and that outside differences shouldn't affect how you feel about a person.

End the activity by putting a happy face symbol on the clusters of things that are alike and different about people to show that both kinds of attributes are good.

—SAMMY'S FIRST DAY—

Read the following story to children.

> Sammy is a new boy in school. He and his mother just moved to the neighborhood, and today is his first day in his new school. Sammy is very short. He has very pale skin and light blue eyes.
>
> When the teacher introduced Sammy to the class, she asked him to tell the class something about himself.
>
> "I like to play the piano," Sammy said. "I live with my mother and my grandpa."
>
> At recess time, Sammy followed the class to the playground. Joey and Steve, the best athletes in the class, decided that Sammy was too small to play ball with them. Maria and Keiko thought it was funny that Sammy didn't have a father at home. They started to laugh at him. Juan and Anthony decided that Sammy was a sissy, because he had such pale skin. They started to call him "Sissy Sammy."

Tell children that Sammy has only been in the new school for two hours and already many children have shown prejudice toward him. Ask the following questions:

❦ Was it fair for Joey and Steve not to ask Sammy to play ball with them just because he was small?

❦ Was it kind of Maria and Keiko to laugh at Sammy because he doesn't live with his father?

❦ Does having pale skin mean that Sammy is a sissy?

❦ How do you think Sammy feels about his new school and himself when these things happen to him?

❦ Is it fair for Sammy's classmates to make judgments about him before they get to know him?

Tell children that what happened to Sammy is called *prejudice*. Prejudice happens when people decide to like or dislike other people before they get to know them. People who are prejudiced may call others names, may not let others play in their games, or may tell mean or ugly stories about others.

Remind children that differences make people interesting. Point out that they wouldn't like to have prejudice happen to them because of their differences. Remind them that they need to treat others the way they would like to be treated. Emphasize that we should show respect for all people.

Ask children to describe how they would welcome Sammy as the new boy in the class.

—THE KIDS WE SEE ON TV—

Videotape a children's television show that features children of the same age as your students. Show children the tape. Then ask children if they saw many different body shapes and sizes in the show.

If the children in the taped show were all about the same size, which is likely to be the case, ask children to think about how they would feel if they were in the show, but had a different body shape or were different in some other way. Would they feel bad or unhappy? Would the difference in how they looked make them behave or act differently?

Encourage children to compose a letter to the producers of the television show to tell them how they feel when they only see one size or type of children on television. Mail the letters after you have made a copy to share with parents (with students' permission).

For Children Ages Eight to Ten

—DEFINING DIVERSITY—

Write the word *diversity* on the board. Ask children to define the word. A good definition would be that diversity is about differences—all of the things that make a person one of a kind, unique.

Ask children to think of examples of how each of them is different. Possible differences include:
- family backgrounds
- likes and dislikes
- physical appearance (skin, hair and eye color; body shape and size; hand and foot size)

- personal qualities (sense of humor, honesty, creativity)
- responses and feelings (feeling angry or sad in the same situation)
- skills and abilities (athletic, musical, artistic)

Tell children that each one of them is different and special—unique. However, they are all alike in many important ways, too. Explain that we are all people, we live together in a society, and we need to help take care of each other. Encourage children to respect and value both the ways they are different and the ways they are the same.

—INVENT A PERSON—

Ask children to draw a picture of a person their age and write a short story about the person's unique qualities. Encourage children to try to make their people different. Tell them to end their stories with a positive statement about their made-up person. For example: He is lots of fun. She is a nice person. He is a good friend.

When children have finished, have them show their pictures and describe the unique qualities of their creations. When all of the invented people have been exhibited, ask children, "Would your person want to feel wanted? Would he or she want to have friends? Would she or he want to enjoy life?" Summarize children's answers by concluding that even though we are different, we are all alike, too.

—Body Image, Then and Now—

Have children look at pictures of people from different times in history in books or works of art. Help them pick out features that made people attractive at that time, such as red hair, a full beard, tiny feet, or a full, round body size (e.g., Rubens' subjects). Tell children that these features were considered beautiful in the past.

Have children look at modern magazines to see if they can find the same attributes (i.e., tiny feet, large body size, etc.). Ask children to discuss or write about why thinness seems to be such an important element of beauty in our current culture.

Ask children to fantasize about what might be considered beautiful in the year 2020. Have them make drawings of what a beautiful person of the year 2020 will look like.

—Skin Deep?—

Suggest that children decide for themselves whether the things that they look at on the outside of people determine what people are like on the inside. Ask them to rewrite the phrase "Beauty is only skin deep" in their own words.

—If We Were All the Same—

Write the question "What would the world be like if everyone looked the same?" on the board. Allow children to write anonymous answers to the question on the board for a few days. When the board is full, read their answers and summarize them in a discussion of personal attitudes and responses to variations in physical appearance.

—What Is Prejudice?—

Have a child read aloud the definition of the word *prejudice* from the dictionary. The definition will be similar to the following: *an opinion or judgment, favorable or more often unfavorable, conceived without proof or competent evidence; a bias against race, religion, background or physical differences.*

Ask children whether people are born prejudiced (no). Discuss the factors that influence our opinions and ask children to give some examples. Factors that influence us include:

- Other people—If family members, peers or people we look up to say something about a person or group of people, we tend to accept it as true.

- Our own experiences—If we have a bad experience with one person of a particular type or group, we may decide that everyone of that group is the same.

- TV, movies and books—These can have a strong influence on our perceptions. For example, if leading characters on TV and in the movies are usually young, thin, White males, we may start to think that only young, thin, White males have exciting and important things to do.

- Poor self-esteem—Some people don't have good opinions of themselves, so they make themselves feel more important by calling other people names and looking down on them.

—What Are Stereotypes?—

Ask a child to read the definition of the word *stereotype* from the dictionary. One definition is *a typical image or concept held by or applied to a certain group.* Ask children to name some stereotypes. Discuss whether the stereotypes are accurate. Ask children to think of and write other stereotypes on a piece of paper. Divide the class into small groups to discuss why stereotypes are not fair.

—Analyzing Advertising—

Collect advertisements for clothes, food or cigarettes from popular magazines. Make a collage of the females and males shown in the ads. Ask children to circle the pictures of any people who are different from the other models in size or other physical characteristics. Discuss the characteristics typically seen in the models who are used in advertisements.

Ask children to analyze the advertisements to determine their truthfulness and honesty. Ask the following questions:

- Will that cosmetic, food or cigarette really make you look like the person in the ad?

- Would you be a better person if you looked like the model and used the product?

- Would your life change if you could magically make yourself look just like the model?

Display the collage for other children in the school to see. Label the stereotypes that are shown.

Classroom Activities to Enhance Self-Esteem*

Recently there has been much discussion about self-esteem in the school setting. Is it teachable, or can it be gained through a conscientious effort by school staff to create an environment where it is enhanced?

Self-esteem is the product of the individual's perception of personal relationships and the experiences that the individual has at home and in school. It can be discussed at the cognitive level and enhanced by a positive environment at school. Self-esteem is about feeling satisfied. Therefore, the goal of self-esteem work is to produce learning situations in which children experience a high level of personal satisfaction while they are learning.

For Children Ages Five to Seven

—HELPING OTHERS—

Ask children how they feel when they've done something good for someone else. Tell children that we can often help ourselves feel better by helping others. Ask children to brainstorm some ideas of things they can do for others. List them on the board.

---

*Some activities in this section are adapted with permission from *The Four Conditions of Self-Esteem: A New Approach for Elementary and Middle Schools* by Reynold Bean, Santa Cruz, CA: ETR Associates, 1992, and from *Smiling at Yourself: Educating Young Children About Stress and Self-Esteem* by Allen N. Mendler, Santa Cruz, CA: ETR Associates, 1991.

In this discussion of others, be sure variation in body size is represented. The differences don't have to be specifically stated, but be sure that the individuals children talk about do vary in size, age, ethnic and cultural background.

Then have children choose one thing they can do to help another person and make a plan to do it. Tell them to draw a picture of the way they are going to help someone.

—What Is a Friend?—

Discuss questions such as What is a friend? What do you like to do with your friend? What does a good friend do? What do I do to be a good friend? Have children write their answers or draw pictures to illustrate them. Display the responses in an area where all classes can enjoy them.

—School Pen Pals—

Set up cross-age friendships by having students in a lower grade class become pen pals with students in an upper grade class. The friends can spend time reading or doing favorite school activities together.

—Personal Badges—

Have children make badges that represent or describe themselves. Tell them the badges can show some of the special things about themselves that make them different from anyone else, the things that make them unique. Encourage children to view body size as a unique and positive characteristic.

Provide a heavy material for the badges, so they will last. Allow children to wear them in class and around the school. Encourage children to use different sizes, shapes and colors for their badges.

—MY FAVORITE ACTIVITY—

Give children the opportunity to choose special projects based on their own interests, hobbies and out-of-school activities. Ask them to prepare a presentation for the class about one of their favorite activities.

—CLASS MANAGER—

Give one child at a time the opportunity to be the class "manager." Allow the manager for the day to select the game at recess, select some of the activities in the classroom, choose a special snack, have some influence over discipline, etc.

Be sure to choose a variety of children to be manager, including children with a variety of body sizes. Some children may need help making decisions as the class manager.

—SPECIAL GUESTS—

Invite special visitors to the classroom to talk to the children about their special skills or hobbies. Invite local athletes, perhaps older student athletes, to talk to the class about how they stay fit. Be sure to choose visitors who will be sensitive to body image issues. Try to find models who represent a variety of racial, ethnic and cultural backgrounds, as well as a variety of body sizes and abilities.

For Children Ages Eight to Ten

—A Class Party—

Have children plan and prepare a class party. Suggest that they plan a party that features healthy snacks. (See Appendix C for some healthy snack suggestions.)

—We Are a Team—

Divide the class into teams of four or five students. Tell teams to make a list of the things the team members have in common. Suggest some possible common factors—family life, clothing, ethnicity, sports, likes and dislikes, homes.

Have teams report to the class. Give each team a prize for some aspect of its report, e.g., most items, most unusual item, most family items. Post the lists in the classroom, and use the items as the basis for spelling exercises if desired.

—My Heritage—

Have children investigate their heritage and prepare reports. Post a large world map in the classroom, so children can indicate their origins on it. Discuss commonalities in background and different cultural attitudes about body size and other physical characteristics.

—Personal Planets—

Have children create personal planets. You might suggest that they create a planet for the unique person they created earlier (see "Invent a Person," p. 52). Tell them they can have anything they want on their planet. Let children describe their planets in words or pictures or make models of them. This activity can be integrated into geography or history by having children create geographies and histories for their planets.

—How Do I Feel?—

Make a list of emotions (anger, fear, love, friendliness, happiness, frustration). Pick one of the emotions and discuss it with children. Have children write something on a long piece of butcher paper about when they feel that way. Decorate the paper and display it in the room. Repeat the activity occasionally with different emotions.

—Radio Shows—

Have children work in small groups to develop, write and produce radio shows that can be used in other classes as learning activities. Have them audiotape the shows.

Children can use seasonal or holiday themes. The shows can include original works, dramatic readings, music, etc. Have students read their own works to create an audiotape library for the classroom.

—Physical Activity Logs—

Have children keep logs of their accomplishments in physical activities. Encourage personal improvement rather than competition. Use activities that even children who feel unathletic can do.

—A Day in the Future—

Pick a date in the future when the children in your class will be grown up. Tell children to write a diary of their activities for the day. Tell them to include such information as their age, their family lives, where they live and what type of work they do.

—Class Goals—

Discuss the importance of personal and group goals. Talk about what goals are, how to set goals and how to make plans to achieve them. Have children write their personal and school goals in a journal.

Have the class discuss and reach consensus on class goals. Post the goals that are agreed on and evaluate the progress toward them periodically. Teach children how to create new goals when the old ones have been reached.

—How to Relax—

Teach children how to relax and relieve stress through managing physical stress in their bodies. Before and after intensive desk work, have children shake out their tensions by jumping in place and shaking their bodies vigorously.

Teach children some body relaxation techniques. Have them learn to tense and relax their limbs and other parts of their bodies to sense when they are tense. Add this approach to lessons on nutrition, the body, art, and all activities in which physical dexterity is useful.

Classroom Activities on Nutrition

Activities that emphasize the basics of good nutrition can help children develop healthy eating habits. As children come to understand the relationship between what they feed their bodies and how their bodies look and perform, they can begin to take responsibility for keeping their bodies healthy by choosing nutritious foods.

For Children Ages Five to Seven

—WATCH OUT FOR FAT—

Discuss guidelines for healthy eating with children. Explain that to be healthy and strong and to stay that way for a lifetime, we need to eat foods that are low in sugar, low in fat and full of fiber. Good examples of these foods are fruits, vegetables and grains.

Teach children to identify the fat content of food by rubbing a piece of the food with a paper towel. If the towel gets a greasy spot on it that doesn't dry or go away, that means the food is high in fat and should be eaten only in small amounts.

Test the following foods: potato chip, apple, peanut butter, hot dog, pretzel, donut, butter, bread, carrot, French fry, and any other foods that are easy to bring into the classroom.

Make lists of foods that we should eat a lot of and foods that we should only eat now and then because of their high fat content. Have children make a poster titled "Eat Lots of These Foods," showing foods high in nutrient density. Arrange for the poster to be displayed in the school cafeteria or lunch area.

For Children Ages Eight to Ten

—Food Is Fuel—

Show children a picture of a car. Ask them to tell you what they know about what makes a car run well. The list should include the need for fuel and maintenance.

Make a chart with the car picture on one side and a stick figure of a person on the other. Under the car picture list the items the children said a car needed to keep running. Under the stick figure let children list similar things that the human body needs to run. Lead children to conclude that the car uses gasoline for fuel while the human body uses food for fuel.

Ask if all gasoline is the same. Explain that there are different kinds of gasoline and that each kind will make a difference in the way the car runs. Tell children the same is true of the food we eat. Add that it is important to give our bodies healthy foods (good fuel) so they will run well.

—THE RIGHT KIND OF FUEL—

Write the word *nutrients* on the board. Explain that nutrients are the things in food that help the body grow. Tell children that some foods are high in nutrients and give the body a lot of energy. Other foods are low in nutrients and give little energy.

Give children some examples of foods with high nutrient density and low nutrient density.

High Nutrient Density	Low Nutrient Density
celery	butter
nonfat milk	milkshake
popcorn without butter	potato chips

Tell children the major difference between the lists is that the high nutrient density foods have no fat content while the low nutrient density foods have fat in them naturally or have had fat added in the preparation process. Talk about where the fat came from in the low nutrient density foods.

Direct students' attention to the chart of car and human needs (see the "Food Is Fuel" activity) and ask what happens if the car or the human takes in too much fuel. The car can't do it (extra fuel spills), but the human can. Explain that when the body takes in more food fuel than it can use, the extra fuel is stored in the body as fat. Too much stored fat is not good for the body.

Tell children that energy balance is the goal. A car maintains a perfect energy balance; it will power itself with the gasoline fuel that has been put into it. A human body is different, because it can store excess energy in fat cells. It can also run on a deficit when there is starvation—but not very efficiently or for very long.

Emphasize that for our bodies, we need to monitor the amount of energy coming in and be sure that it is of high nutrient density. We also need to keep active so the body will burn off the energy it takes in and not store too much as fat.

Classroom Activities to Encourage Physical Activity

Activities that emphasize physical activity can help all children feel good about moving their bodies and help them appreciate the need for regular, vigorous physical activity.

—COLLAGE OF ATHLETES—

Decorate the walls of the school gym or multipurpose room with a mural or collage of pictures of athletes clipped from newspapers and magazines. Include pictures of male and female athletes, as well as handicapped or wheelchair athletes. Be sure pictures depict athletes of a variety of sizes and shapes and from a variety of ethnic groups. Look for pictures of jockeys, baseball players, basketball players, swimmers, gymnasts and shot putters.

Label the collage with the phrase "These athletes are all fit" to help children realize that successful athletes come in all sizes and shapes.

For Children Ages Five to Seven

—USING MY MUSCLES—

Ask children to move around the room in a circle in a way that uses their body's muscles: skip, jog, pretend to swim, bicycle, jump rope, etc. When children have completed the circle, ask them to stand still and point to the body muscle groups that they used for their activity.

—WHEN YOU EXERCISE—

Ask children to help you make a chart of the good things that happen when you exercise. The chart will include statements such as the following:

- I feel good.

- My muscles get strong.

- My heart works better.

- My muscles stay firm.

- I can think better.

Help children copy the chart to take home. Ask them to decorate their charts with drawings of themselves doing their favorite physical activities.

For Children Ages Eight to Ten

—Discussing Activity—

Discuss the value and benefits of physical activity (feel healthier, have stronger muscles, heart is stronger, cope with stress). Teach children a fitness vocabulary that includes the terms *cardiovascular fitness, muscular strength,* and *flexibility.*

Use definitions similar to the following:

- Cardiovascular fitness refers to the ability of the heart and lungs to do their work.

- Muscular strength refers to the ability of the muscles to do their work.

- Flexibility refers to the ability of the body's joints to move through a full range of motion.

Ask children to think about factors that help us decide what activities we will participate in. What kinds of activities might enhance the different types of fitness? Discuss children's ideas.

—A Wall Walk—

Involve children in a classroom physical fitness activity called a "wall walk." Have children make drawings of one of their shoes and put their names on the shoes. Make a shoe for yourself, too.

Make a line graph with numbers from one to fifty, and post it on the classroom wall. Tape the shoes to the graph. Put all of the shoes at the number one. Tell children they are going to use the graph to keep track of the number of times they walk the circumference of the playground.

Take the class to the playground for a walk around it. Complete as many full circles around the playground as time allows. Back in the classroom, move the shoes to show the number of laps each child walked.

Continue the activity for several weeks. Take group walks at least two or three times a week, and encourage children to take walks on their own before or after school or during recess. Tell children to move their shoes along the wall walk to indicate the number of laps they have completed. At the end of each week, total the number of laps the class has collectively walked. Send a letter to the school principal that proudly announces the number of laps that have been completed.

This activity makes the simplest form of physical activity fun and noncompetitive and offers all children the chance to succeed at physical activity.

—A Schoolwide Wall Walk—

Invite other members of the school staff to join the wall walk. The nurse, the librarian, the principal, the secretary and the custodian can all have a shoe and can join the class for a lap around the playground. Adult modeling is very important in instilling healthy behaviors in children.

Chapter 6

Handling Difficult
Situations

As caring adults, we try to provide a supportive environment for children, whatever their body size and abilities. However, our best efforts may sometimes be thwarted by encounters with others who are not sensitive to body image issues.

How we deal with these situations will have an impact on children. The following case studies illustrate some constructive responses to these difficult situations.

Janet and Kathy

Janet was not looking forward to the family gathering in honor of her father's sixtieth birthday. In fact, she was dreading it. She could already hear her mother exclaiming, "My goodness, child, you're going to be a giant if you keep on growing at this rate!" as she greeted Janet's daughter, Cindi.

Janet was feeling tense just thinking about how her mother always commented on the fact that Cindi was a larger than average child. As if that wasn't bad enough, Janet's sister, Kathy, was forever pointing out the physical differences between her daughter, Lila, and Cindi.

Lila was a petite, slender ten year old with blue eyes, naturally curly blond hair, and a peaches and cream complexion that was probably pimple-resistant. Janet frowned as she pictured Cindi, with her limp brown hair and pre-adolescent awkwardness, standing next to her beautiful cousin.

The two girls had been born just a couple of months apart, and at first it had been fun sharing parenting experiences with Kathy. Of course, Cindi had grown at a much more rapid rate than Lila, even in infancy.

Initially, this was a source of pride for Janet; her child was big, strong and healthy. However, as the years passed and Cindi continued to grow at a more rapid rate than Lila, Janet found herself worrying rather than rejoicing about the difference.

Janet's husband, John, was a strapping six-footer who looked like a lumberjack but was actually an accountant. Bigness ran in John's family; his sister, Meg, was 5'10", and his brother, Bob, was 6'2".

Cindi looked a lot more like her cousins on John's side of the family. Unfortunately, those cousins lived more than 700 miles away. The families got together for weddings and funerals, but the distance was too great for regular get-togethers.

"I wished we lived closer to John's family," Janet thought, remembering how close she had come to losing her temper at her family's last gathering. Cindi and Lila had asked their mothers if they could have identical dresses for Easter.

"Where in the world do you shop for Cindi's clothes?" Kathy had asked. "Does anything in the pre-teen department fit her?" Then Kathy had told the girls that even though it was a nice idea, it would probably be impossible to find identical dresses in such different sizes.

At that point, the girls' grandmother had graciously offered to sew identical dresses for her two granddaughters.

"Great," Janet had thought sourly. "Now the differences between the two girls will be really obvious."

Stop reading now. Ask yourself:

1. What would you have done if you were Janet?

2. If Janet came to you for advice about handling this difficult situation, what would you advise her to do?

Read on to find out what happened.

The week before her father's sixtieth birthday party, Janet attended a workshop on children and weight led by a registered dietitian. She was surprised by some of the things the dietitian had to say. She also realized that she needed help in handling her sister's constant needling about Cindi's size.

Handling Difficult Situations _____ 71

After the session, Janet went up to talk to the dietitian. She told him that she felt her sister was making too many negative comments about Cindi's size and that it was time to put a stop to it. But she also wanted to maintain a good relationship with Kathy because they had always been close. And she knew that a rift in the sisters' relationship was apt to distress her parents and create family problems.

The dietitian suggested that Janet ask her sister out to lunch, just the two of them. "Start off by telling your sister that you are concerned about Cindi," he said. "Say that you are afraid Cindi is beginning to view her body in a negative way. Ask Kathy to help you in your efforts to help Cindi feel good about herself just the way she is. Then suggest some specific ways Kathy can help."

The next week, Janet met Kathy for lunch. The conversation began just as the dietitian suggested, but things didn't go exactly as planned.

After Janet said her piece, Kathy responded that she would be much more careful about what she said in Cindi's presence. But then she told Janet that, in return, Janet should start treating Lila in a more accepting way.

"Lila has noticed that you never pay any attention to her," Kathy said. "So have Larry and I. Don't you think it hurts Lila to be ignored by her aunt? Besides, you are the one who started comparing the two girls when they were babies. You thought it was great that Cindi was so much bigger than Lila then."

Janet was surprised. She hardly knew what to say. But then she realized that Kathy was right, she had been ignoring Lila. And she had been the one who initiated comparisons of the two cousins.

As she thought about it, Janet realized that she resented Lila because of her appearance. Lila was so pretty. But she wasn't conceited about her appearance; she seemed oblivious to it.

Lila and Cindi were actually best friends. The cousins never seemed to notice that they were quite different physically. Their friendship seemed to be based on mutual affection and respect.

Janet felt depressed as she realized that part of the problem was her own uneasiness about Cindi's body. As a result of her own attitudes, she was overly sensitive to any reference to Cindi's size.

"I've managed to make a real mess of things," Janet thought. But then Kathy reached across the table and took her hand.

"Hey, look," Kathy said. "We can work it out. We've been sisters for over thirty years, and we're going to be sisters for a lot more. Why don't we both turn over a new leaf?"

Janet was relieved. She tightened her grip on her sister's hand and said, "Absolutely." In her mind, she resolved to work on feeling good about her daughter's body and to be a much more loving and affectionate aunt to Lila.

Ask yourself:

1. Are you surprised by what happened?

2. Would you change your earlier advice to Janet?

Read the next case study and think about how you might handle this one.

The Williams Family

Mr. Williams could tell that something was wrong at school the minute he walked into Booker's room. Booker was lying on his back looking at the ceiling. He was usually in the family room in front of the TV when Mr. Williams got home from work.

"Hi, guy! How was your day?" Mr. Williams asked.

"OK," Booker answered in a quivery voice.

"Are you sure?" Mr. Williams asked. "You seem a little depressed to me."

"I hate school!" Booker exclaimed. "Why do I have to go to school?"

"Well, you've learned a lot of things in school," Mr. Williams said, "like how to read and do math. You know, I think something must have happened at school today to make you feel sad and angry. Will you please tell me about it?"

"He didn't let me race."

"Who didn't let you race?"

"Mr. Sullivan."

"Was everybody else racing?"

"Yeah, but not me."

"Can you tell me more about what happened?" Mr. Williams asked. "When was everybody racing, and why were they racing? What exactly did Mr. Sullivan say to you?"

"He said it probably wasn't a good idea for me to race. He said he was afraid I might *overzert* myself. He told me to go sit on the bleachers while everyone else raced."

"You mean *overexert* yourself," Mr. Williams said. "So why was everyone else racing?"

"Mr. Sullivan needed to know how long it took everybody to run a mile. We all went across the street to that track behind the junior high school. And he told everyone to line up along the starting line.

"And so I went over and stood on the line, but then he came over and told me to go sit on the bleachers. Then he yelled, 'Go' and everyone else ran around the track as fast as they could, except me."

"I bet you felt really bad about being left out."

"He just thinks because I'm big, I can't run. But I can run! I bet I could have beat a lot of those guys if he'd let me run!"

"I bet you could have, too. I think you're right to feel upset about being made to sit on the bleachers while everyone else was racing."

Later in the evening, as Mr. Williams talked to his wife about what had happened to Booker, he found himself getting angrier and angrier. This wasn't the first time Booker had been treated differently from everyone else.

A couple of weeks before, he had come home from the class Halloween party and complained that everyone had gotten a chocolate chip cookie decorated with M&M's except him. He got a cookie, but it didn't have M&M's on it.

Another time, Booker had complained that the kids were teasing him and calling him names like "blobman" and "fatsit." Booker said Mr. Sullivan had overheard them, but he just told them to sit down and start doing their work.

Booker also said that Mr. Sullivan hardly ever called on him when he raised his hand. "Mr. Sullivan probably thinks I'm dumb because I'm big," Booker had added.

"It's just not fair!" Mr. Williams stormed to his wife. "That teacher is treating Booker differently just because he's large. I'm going over to that school tomorrow and give him a piece of my mind! And I'm going to tell him that if he doesn't change his ways, the next time I'm going straight to the principal! And after that I'm going to the board of education! I'm not going to let him get away with this!"

Stop reading now. Ask yourself:

If you were Mrs. Williams, what would you say to your husband?

Read on to find out what happened.

Mrs. Williams listened to her husband, and then said, "Do you really think that's going to help—going up there and yelling at the teacher?"

"I didn't say I was going to yell at him," Mr. Williams responded. "I'm just going to tell him that he is being unfair to Booker and that he had better watch his step from now on."

"Sounds pretty threatening to me," Mrs. Williams said.

"Well, what would you suggest—that I go up there on my hands and knees and beg him to treat Booker fairly?"

"No, of course not. I was just thinking that maybe we could get him on our side, ask him to help Booker feel better about himself. Maybe Mr. Sullivan could help Booker see himself the way we do—as a great kid who just happens to be the biggest boy in the fifth grade, rather than as a social outcast who doesn't fit in."

"I suppose you're right," Mr. Williams said, "I could probably handle this in a more constructive way. I guess I'm letting my anger get the best of me."

"Look, why don't we both go up there?" Mrs. Williams suggested. "I'll explain to Mr. Sullivan that we're both worried about the way Booker sees himself and that we want him to feel good about himself. He's one heck of a good kid, who just happens to be extra big."

"Yeah," Mr. Williams said, "I remember that I was always the biggest boy in my class in grammar school, but my teachers always acted like that was a plus. They'd ask me to help them carry stuff to and from their cars before and after school.

"Why, I remember my fifth grade teacher saying that it was

wonderful having someone who was so strong around to help out. I always felt that being big was great.

"I'm glad you're going to go with me," he added. "I think teachers pay more attention when both parents are there. Plus, you don't get angry the way I do. I am apt to fly off the handle. And you're right, that wouldn't help the situation and might even make it worse. Mr. Sullivan might get angry at me and take it out on Booker."

The following morning, Mr. Williams called Mr. Sullivan and made arrangements for an after-school meeting. When Mr. and Mrs. Williams arrived at the classroom, Mr. Sullivan was waiting for them, along with the school nurse, Ms. Velasco.

Mr. Williams explained why they had arranged to meet with Mr. Sullivan; they wanted him to help Booker improve his body image. Ms. Velasco immediately spoke up and said that Booker was too fat and shouldn't gain any more weight until he had grown into his current weight.

She added that Booker should spend less time in front of the television set and more time playing actively. She then gave Mr. and Mrs. Williams a mini-lecture on good nutrition, insisting that the family adopt a sensible low-fat diet.

Mrs. Williams could see that her husband was becoming upset. As soon as Ms. Velasco had finished, Mrs. Williams said, "I can see that we all have the same goal in mind—helping Booker. If my husband and I start doing some of the things you've suggested in terms of improving our eating habits, will the two of you work on helping Booker improve his body image and his self-esteem?"

"Yes," Mr. Sullivan responded immediately. "I know that Booker feels bad about being the biggest child in the fifth grade, and I promise that I will help him as well as the rest of the children treat each other's bodies with respect.

"I've heard the other children teasing Booker," he added. "I've usually just diverted their attention to something else, but now I think we'll have a classroom discussion about size diversity and the need to respect the bodies of others."

"That sounds wonderful," Mrs. Williams said. "We really appreciate your help."

Ms. Velasco then gave Mrs. Williams a pamphlet on the U.S. Dietary Guidelines. Mrs. Williams politely said she would read it, even though she felt the family already ate nutritious food. The meeting ended fairly amicably.

Ask yourself:

1. Are you surprised by what happened?

2. How would you have responded to Ms. Velasco's lecture?

3. Would you change your earlier advice to Mr. Williams?

Read the next case study, from a teacher's viewpoint, and think about how you might handle this one.

Ms. Wong and Sara

Ms. Wong knew that Sara's parents were divorced because there were different addresses listed for them on the school roster. She wasn't too surprised when they made separate appointments to see her a few months into the school year. Sara's mother, Karen Brown, had an appointment a few days before Sara's father's appointment.

"I do hope my ugly duckling is finally going to blossom this year," Ms. Brown said at the beginning of the discussion. "It seems like she's been going through an awkward phase her entire childhood. She's all hands and legs. I keep telling her that one day she will turn into a beautiful swan, but I'm a little worried that it may never happen! What do you think?"

Stop reading now. Ask yourself:

If you were Ms. Wong, what would you say to Karen's mother?

Read on to find out what happened.

"Well, I've never really given much thought to Sara's physical appearance," Ms. Wong replied. "She looks like most fourth-grade girls. She *is* tall. I guess she's the tallest girl in the class this year, but I've had taller girls other years. As far as coordination goes, I'd say her coordination is in the average range."

"Yes, but average is just average," Ms. Brown said. "I want Sara to be far above average in everything."

"Well, she certainly is above average in some areas," Ms. Wong said. "For example, she is very good at math and science."

"Isn't that amazing!" Ms. Brown exclaimed. "I can't even keep my checkbook straight.

"You do know that Sara's father walked out on us last year?" she added. "He just came home one day and said that our marriage wasn't working. You could have knocked me over with a feather. I never had any inkling that he was unhappy."

"How did Sara feel when her dad left?"

"Oh, she was crushed, but she just had to get used to it, like I did. I even had to find a job. Let me tell you, that wasn't easy after staying home for twelve years. Of course, I really didn't stay at home. Between tennis, bridge, golf and volunteer work, I was always busy.

"But I had to give it all up. Well, almost all...I do manage to play golf and tennis on the weekends. But I can't play bridge every Thursday afternoon the way I used to, and I certainly don't have time for volunteer work. Now I have to work for money."

"Does Sara ever play tennis or golf with you?" Ms. Wong asked, trying to refocus the conversation on Sara.

"Goodness no, she's far too uncoordinated to do either. Anyway, she spends the weekends with her father."

"I really don't think Sara is uncoordinated," Ms. Wong said. "With some practice, she might actually become a good athlete."

"Do you really think so? Well, I can't afford tennis or golf lessons. Perhaps you could ask her father if he could pay for them?"

"I really don't think that would be appropriate. However, I do know that the parks and recreation department offers sports lessons after school and during the summer for nominal fees. I have their phone number; let me get it for you."

As the meeting ended, Ms. Brown promised that she would call parks and recreation about their after-school programs and might possibly sign Sara up for something.

Ms. Wong hoped that in some small way she had changed Ms. Brown's opinion about Sara. It was sad to hear Sara's mother refer to her as an ugly duckling.

The meeting with Sara's father was more positive, however. Mr. Brown never mentioned the fact that Sara was a tall, gangly child. He was more interested in her academic performance. He was also concerned that the divorce had affected Sara in a negative way. Her grades had gone down. She seemed sad and depressed a lot of the time.

Ms. Wong was able to suggest some ways Mr. Brown could help Sara during this difficult period. She also brought up the fact that Sara was very reluctant to participate in physical education activities. She always had some reason for being excused from P.E.

"Somehow, Sara has come to the conclusion that she isn't good at sports and never will be," Ms. Wong said. "It's true, she is a little awkward, but with practice she could develop her skills."

"Is there some way I could help her?" Mr. Brown asked.

"Do you ever take her bike riding? play ball with her? go swimming?"

"Gee, no, but we certainly could start doing those things," Mr. Brown said.

"I think that would help. Don't expect too much of her, just let her enjoy using her body. And be sure to praise her for her willingness to try to learn new skills," Ms. Wong advised.

At the end of the meeting, Ms. Wong felt reassured that Sara's dad was going to make a concerted effort to help his daughter improve her sports skills.

Ms. Wong also talked to the P.E. teacher. She explained that Sara was afraid of participating in P.E. because she didn't feel that her body would perform adequately. The P.E. teacher promised to make a special effort to spend time on skills development before initiating sports activities. This eventually helped Sara, and a number of other children, to feel more confident about their physical competence.

Ask yourself:

1. If Ms. Wong came to you for a critique of this situation, what would you say to her?

2. Would you suggest any follow-up on her meetings with Sara's parents?

Guidelines to Follow

The following guidelines are important to keep in mind when expressing your concerns to others who work with the child.

Focus on Helping the Child

Your reason for dealing with the situation is to help the child. Keep reminding yourself and others of this. Don't be diverted by other issues. Always bring the conversation back to focus on this goal.

Evaluate how things are going in terms of whether you are achieving this goal. Mrs. Williams was very effective at keeping the focus on ways to help Booker during the meeting with Mr. Sullivan and Ms. Velasco.

Don't Create a Confrontation

How might Kathy have reacted if Janet had started off by saying, "You are always making negative comments about Cindi's size, and I would like you to stop"? When you confront people, they feel threatened and may hear very little of what you have to say. They focus on the fact that you are angry with them.

Ask for Assistance

If you want someone to help a child feel good about his or her body, ask for assistance in a simple, straightforward manner. Don't be reluctant to state the problem clearly. For example,

"Sara feels that she is uncoordinated. She doesn't trust her body so she is afraid to use it. I am asking you to help her have a more positive body image."

People are usually very responsive to requests for assistance. Everyone likes to be viewed as a capable, helpful person.

Suggest Positive Ways to Help

You can begin the conversation in a general way, but be prepared to describe specific ways in which others can help. For example, Janet could have said to Kathy, "Ask Cindi to tell you about the history project she did for school. She got an *A* on it, and I know she's very proud of this accomplishment."

People want to help but they aren't always sure how to help. Be prepared to give them specific suggestions, such as those Ms. Wong gave Sara's parents.

Don't List Past Grievances

When you list all the things that have annoyed you in the past, people feel the need to explain why they took the actions they did. They may also want to justify each of their actions.

What if Mr. Williams had listed all of the ways in which he felt Mr. Sullivan had discriminated against Booker because of his large size? Mr. Sullivan might have felt the need to explain what had happened with respect to each situation. It would have been very difficult to refocus the conversation on helping Booker after reviewing a litany of complaints.

Be Open to Suggestions

Other people may have their own opinions about how your child can be helped. For example, Mr. Sullivan thought Booker could benefit from eating low-fat meals and snacks, so he asked the school nurse to attend the meeting with Booker's parents. He felt the nurse knew more about diet and health than he did and would do a better job of explaining the changes that needed to be made.

Booker's parents arrived at the meeting with a completely different agenda, but they politely listened to what Ms. Velasco had to say. Then Booker's mom suggested a solution that blended the two approaches and kept the focus on helping Booker.

Be at Your Mature, Reasonable Best

Before you deal with a difficult situation, tell yourself that you are going to deal with it in a way that will make you proud of yourself. You will be cordial in approaching the other person. You will be reasonable in terms of what you ask the person to do. You will remain calm throughout.

Mr. Williams knew that he flew off the handle easily, so he remained quiet and let his wife respond to Mr. Sullivan and Ms. Velasco.

Expect the Unexpected

Mentally rehearsing how to handle a situation can be helpful. It's good to think about how to approach someone in a tactful manner. But also realize that things don't usually happen exactly as you imagine they will. Be ready for the unexpected.

Janet was surprised when her sister brought up the fact that she was ignoring her niece. Fortunately, Janet did not react defensively. Instead, she accepted responsibility for this behavior and decided to change.

❧ ❧ ❧

Teachers, parents and other caregivers may have to deal with difficult situations when they are concerned about a child's poor body image. When you find yourself faced with such a situation, think about how you can use the techniques described in this chapter to best help the child.

Appendix A

Assessing Children's Growth

Because there is so much variability in children's growth, there are no ideal height-weight tables for children. Instead, health professionals plot children's height and weight throughout infancy, childhood and adolescence on growth charts. It is also common to plot head circumference during infancy to measure brain growth.

The charts that are used for plotting these measurements are standard charts developed by the National Center for Health Statistics. (See Tables 1, 2, 3 and 4.) They are based on a large-scale survey of a cross section of the pediatric population conducted in the late 1960s and early 1970s.

There are different charts for girls and boys. There are charts for birth to 36 months and for ages two to eighteen. There are also special charts for prepubescence, when growth is quite rapid. It is very important to use the right chart when plotting height and weight.

It is also important to use the right tools to measure height and weight. Children younger than two years old will be measured while lying down. A special measuring board is used to take this measurement. After two years of age, children are usually measured standing, using an accurate measuring instrument.

Balance beam scales are used to obtain accurate weights. Balance beam scales are available for home use, but they are quite expensive. Most standard scales sold for home use are considered unreliable indicators of accurate weight.

Health professionals assess a child's growth by plotting height and weight measurements over time. A child will establish his or her own growth curve on the NCHS growth chart. It is very difficult to tell whether a child is growing normally by taking measurements at one point in time. Health professionals need to have the child's measurements from birth onward to accurately assess growth.

Almost all pediatricians will track a child's growth on the NCHS growth charts from birth onward. These charts become a standard part of a child's medical history. If a family moves or changes pediatricians, the child's medical records should be forwarded to the new pediatrician. Pediatricians, pediatric registered nurses and pediatric registered dietitians are all capable of assessing children's growth to determine whether it is normal. Remember, there is a wide range of what is considered normal.

Measurements that fall between the 5th and 95th percentiles on the growth charts are usually considered normal. Measurements below the 5th percentile and above the 95th percentile may or may not be normal; the child's growth history is required to make this determination.

Dramatic shifts in measurements between percentiles or above the 95th percentile may indicate impending obesity. Individuals with training in child growth and development should make this determination. If you have concerns about a child's weight, consult an expert.

Certain diseases can cause short stature in children because they alter the body's ability to digest, absorb or use nutrients from food. Examples of these diseases are inflammatory bowel disease, chronic kidney disease, chronic lung disease, diabetes, liver disease and heart disease. All of these diseases are chronic in that they persist over a long period of time, often lasting years or even a lifetime.

Short height is also associated with other physical problems such as skeletal disorders, chromosomal abnormalities, mental retardation and hormonal disorders. Hormonal disorders can be effectively treated, but the other problems cannot.

Excessive tallness can also be caused by organic diseases, including Marfan's syndrome, homocystinuria, a pituitary tumor, cerebral gigantism, hyperthyroidism, sexual precocity, testicular feminization syndrome and XXY or XYY karotype.

Treatment of extreme shortness or tallness is somewhat controversial because it involves the administration of hormones that can cause negative side effects. Diagnosis and treatment of these problems should be done by an endocrinologist, a medical doctor who specializes in the diagnosis and treatment of glandular disorders.

Boys from 2 to 18 years

Stature for Age

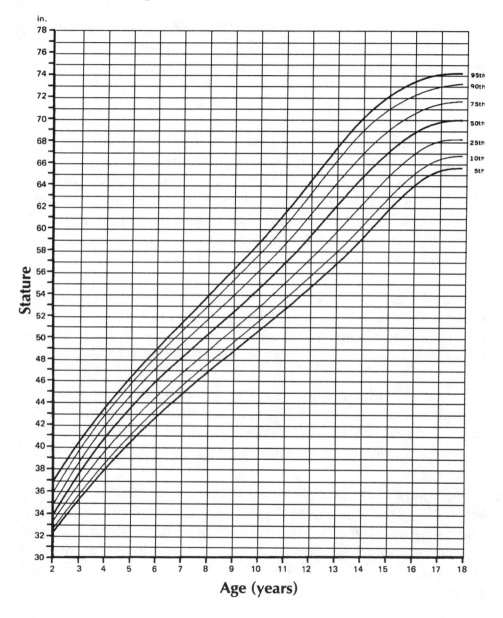

Am I Fat?

Boys from 2 to 18 years

Weight for Age

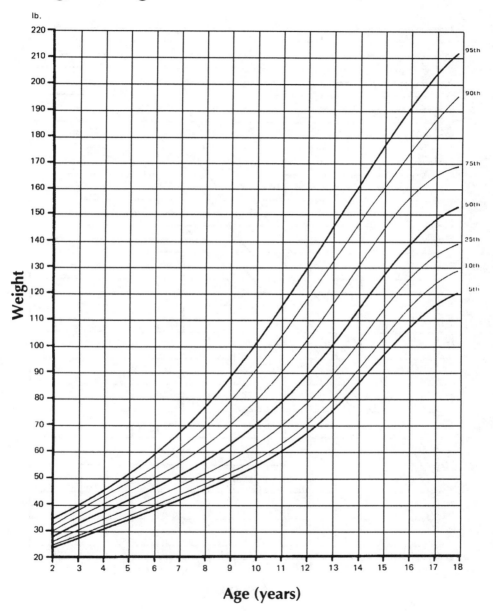

Age (years)

Girls from 2 to 18 years

Stature for Age

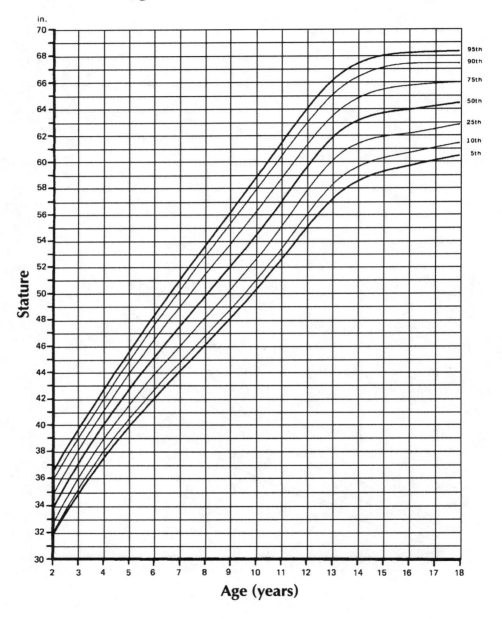

_____ *Am I Fat?*

Girls from 2 to 18 years

Weight for Age

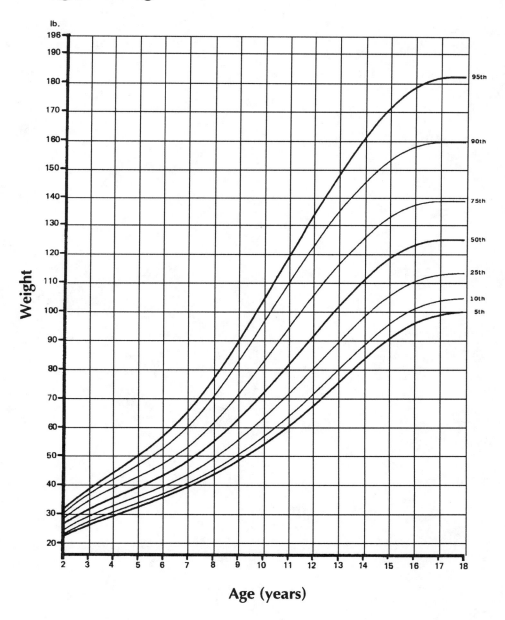

Age (years)

Appendix B

Nutrient Density of Foods

Breads, Cereals and Other Grain Products

High Nutrient Density	Good Nutrient Density	Lower Nutrient Density
Bagels	Biscuits	Ready-to-eat sugared cereals
Bread sticks	Quick breads	Corn chips
Whole grain or enriched breads	Graham crackers	Tortilla chips
English muffins	Oyster crackers	Cheese crackers
Cooked cereals	Granola	Snack crackers
Ready-to-eat unsugared cereals	Pancakes	Croissants
Grits, boiled	Pretzels	Doughnuts
Macaroni	Saltines	Granola bars
Matzo	Waffles	Fried grits
Noodles		Pastries
Pita bread		Sweet rolls
Rice (white and brown)		
Spaghetti		
Tortillas (flour or corn)		

Fruits and Vegetables

High Nutrient Density	Good Nutrient Density	Lower Nutrient Density
All fresh fruits and vegetables Fruits canned in juice Frozen fruit-juice bars Fruit juices Vegetable juices Canned vegetables Plain frozen vegetables Soups, including cream soups made with nonfat milk	Fruits canned in light syrup	French fries Fruits canned in heavy syrup Frozen fruit-flavored bars Pickles, olives, hash-browns Vegetables frozen with butter or other sauce

Milk and Milk Products

High Nutrient Density	Good Nutrient Density	Lower Nutrient Density
Buttermilk made from skim or low-fat milk Low-fat cheeses such as ricotta and mozzarella Low-fat cottage cheese Low-fat milk Nonfat milk Nonfat or low-fat dry milk	Cheese made with whole milk "Light" ice cream (7% fat) Ice milk Whole milk Pudding made with nonfat milk Sherbet Frozen yogurt	Cream cheese Heavy cream Whipped cream Half and half Ice cream Chocolate milk Sour cream

Meat, Poultry, Fish, Eggs, Beans and Nuts

High Nutrient Density	Good Nutrient Density	Lower Nutrient Density
Almonds, beech-nuts, Brazil nuts, filberts, pecans, walnuts Beans Well-trimmed, lean cuts of beef, pork, veal and lamb Chicken and turkey without skin, including ground turkey Fish and shellfish (other than fried) Hamburger (made from a lean cut such as the beef round) Peas (split, chick, black-eyed) Pumpkin and sunflower seeds Refried beans made without lard Tuna canned in water	Eggs Peanut butter Peanuts, pista-chios, cashews, macadamia nuts	Bacon Bologna Chitterlings Corned beef Deep-fried chicken Deep-fried fish Frankfurters Hamburger or regular ground beef Refried beans made with lard Salami Sausage Tuna canned in oil

Sweets, Fats and Snack Foods

Low Nutrient Density (Use in moderation.)	Low Nutrient Density (Use rarely.)
Cookies Diet margarine Diet soft drinks Margarine Mayonnaise Salad dressings made with oil Vegetable oils	Butter Candy Chocolate Corn chips Fruit-flavored drinks Soft drinks Gravies Ham hocks Honey Jelly, jam, marmalade Lard Potato chips Salad dressing made with sour cream or cheese Salt pork Rich sauces Sugar

Appendix C

Snacks with Kid Appeal

Are there snacks that kids like that are nutrient dense? Yes, yes, yes! There are lots of good-for-you snacks that have "kid appeal." Most children who are eight years old can easily prepare the following snacks without adult supervision. They're written in easy-to-follow directions that have been "kid tested." Encourage children to prepare them as after-school snacks.

—FRUIT JUICE POPSICLES—

Use your favorite fruit juices to make yummy popsicles! You will need fruit juice and popsicle molds.

Do this:

1. Pour the fruit juice into the popsicle molds.

2. Put the tops on the molds.

3. Put the molds in the freezer.

4. Wipe up any juice that has spilled. Put leftover juice in the refrigerator.

5. In an hour or two, take a frozen popsicle out of the freezer.

6. Run the mold under warm water for just a few seconds to get the popsicle out.

If you don't have popsicle molds, you can use an ice cube tray to make fruit juice ice cubes to suck on.

—QUESADILLA—

This is a quick, microwave snack for after school. You will need one flour tortilla, grated cheese (any kind you like) or cheese and a grater (if the cheese isn't already grated).

Do this:

1. If the cheese isn't grated, find the grater and grate it. Or cut the cheese in small pieces.

2. Sprinkle the cheese over half of the tortilla.

3. Fold over the half of the tortilla with no cheese on it so that it covers the half with cheese.

4. Put the tortilla on a paper towel. Place the towel and tortilla in the microwave oven.

5. Set the microwave oven to medium for one minute. Now zap it (turn it on) so the cheese melts.

6. While the quesadilla is cooking, wrap up any extra cheese and tortillas. Put them in the refrigerator. Wash the grater or put it in the dishwasher.

7. Take your quesadilla out of the microwave. You can cut it in halves or in thirds, or you can eat it just the way it is. Quesadillas taste great with a glass of milk!

Next time: Add some chopped green chilies, or a little salsa, or chopped black olives on top of the cheese for zippier flavor. Remember, chopped green chilies taste hot and so does salsa. Don't use too much of these unless you like them a lot.

—Mini-Pizzas—

These are an all-time microwave or toaster-oven favorite. You will need one English muffin, pizza sauce (canned or from a jar), grated mozzarella cheese or mozzarella cheese and a grater.

Do this:

1. Split the English muffin in half.

2. Open the jar or can of pizza sauce. Use a spoon to spread pizza sauce on each half of the English muffin.

3. If the cheese isn't grated, find the grater and grate it. Or break the cheese into tiny pieces.

4. Sprinkle the cheese all over the top of the mini-pizzas.

5. Put the pizzas on a paper towel. Place in the microwave oven.

6. Set the microwave oven to medium for one minute. Now zap it (turn it on) so the cheese melts.

7. If you don't have a microwave, put the mini-pizzas in a toaster oven. Toast them until the cheese is all melted.

8. Wrap up any leftover cheese. Put the lid on the jar of pizza sauce. If the pizza sauce came from a can, don't leave it in the can. Put it in a small bowl and cover it. Put the cheese and the leftover sauce in the refrigerator. Wash the grater or put it in the dishwasher.

9. Pour yourself a glass of fruit juice and drink it as you eat your pizza!

More Snacks with Kid Appeal

Here are some additional snacks in the high or good nutrient density categories:

Fresh fruit kabobs—Cut up fruit and skewer it in colorful arrangements.

Low-fat or nonfat frozen yogurt—Check the dairy case at the supermarket. There are lots of appealing fresh fruit flavors available.

Low-fat or nonfat fruit yogurt—Yes, it has some added sugar, but it also is a good source of protein, calcium, phosphorus and riboflavin.

Ready-to-eat cereal—Not all ready-to-eat cereals are high in added sugar. Check the nutrition label on the box. Kids enjoy mixing and munching on ready-to-eat cereals. For variety, add nuts, raisins or other dried fruit to the cereal mixture.

Nuts—Choose almonds, Brazil nuts, filberts, pecans, walnuts, dry roasted unsalted peanuts, pistachios, cashews and macadamia nuts.

Seeds—Sunflower seeds are reasonably priced.

Pudding made with nonfat milk—The milk adds the nutrients and makes it nutritious. Children can make instant pudding by pouring the pudding mix into a jar, adding the correct amount of nonfat milk and then shaking the jar vigorously.

Whole grain crackers, pretzels, bread sticks—Check nutrition labels to select those lower in fat and sodium (salt may be listed as sodium chloride).

Suggested Readings

American Cancer Society. 1990. *Changing the Course: Manual for School Foodservice Providers.* (Available through local ACS offices.)

Bean, R. 1992. *The Four Conditions of Self-Esteem: A New Approach for Elementary and Middle Schools.* Santa Cruz, CA: ETR Associates.

Bennett, J. P., and A. Kamiya. 1986. *Fitness and Fun for Everyone!* Durham, NC: The Great Activities Publishing Company.

Bossenmeyer, M. 1989. *Peaceful Playgrounds: An Elementary Teacher's Guide to Recess Games and Markings.* Byron, CA: Front Row Experience.

Canfield, J. 1986. *Self-Esteem in the Classroom.* Pacific Palisades, CA: Self-Esteem Seminars.

Carnes, C. 1983. *Awesome Elementary School Physical Education Activities.* Carmichael, CA: Author.

Hatfield, E., and S. Sprecher. 1988. *Mirror, Mirror: The Importance of Looks in Everyday Life.* New York: SUNY Press.

Hutchinson, M. G. 1985. *Transforming Body Image.* Trumansburg, NY: The Crossing Press.

Ikeda, J., and R. Mitchell. 1991. *Children and Weight: What's a Parent to Do?* Oakland, CA: University of California Cooperative Extension, Division of Agriculture and Natural Resources.

Ikeda, J. 1991. *Food Choices for Good Health.* Oakland, CA: University of California Cooperative Extension, Division of Agriculture and Natural Resources.

Ikeda, J. 1989. *If My Child Is Too Fat, What Should I Do About It?* Oakland, CA: University of California Cooperative Extension, Division of Agriculture and Natural Resources.

Malone, M. J. 1989. *Kids Weigh to Fitness.* Reston, VA: American Alliance for Health, Physical Education, Recreation and Dance.

Matiella, A. C. 1991. *Positively Different: Creating a Bias-Free Environment for Young Children.* Santa Cruz, CA: ETR Associates.

Mendler, A. N. 1990. *Smiling at Yourself: Educating Young Children About Stress and Self-Esteem.* Santa Cruz, CA: ETR Associates.

Orbach, S. 1978. *Fat Is a Feminist Issue*. New York: Berkeley Books.

Petray, C. K., and S. L. Blazer. 1987. *Health-Related Physical Fitness: Concepts and Activities for Elementary School Chirdren*. 2d ed. Edina, MN: Bellwether Press.

Satter, E. 1987. *How to Get Your Kid to Eat...But Not Too Much*. Palo Alto, CA: Bull Publishing Company.

References

Abbey, N., C. Brindis and M. Casas. 1990. *Family life education in multicultural classrooms: Practical guidelines.* Ed. A. C. Matiella. Santa Cruz, CA: ETR Associates.

Bean, R. 1992. *The four conditions of self-esteem: A new approach for elementary and middle schools.* Santa Cruz, CA: ETR Associates.

Birch, L. L., D. Birch, D. Marlin and L. Kramer. 1982. Effects of instrumental eating on children's food preferences. *Appetite* 3:125-134.

Birch, L. L., and M. Deysher. 1985. Conditioned and unconditioned caloric compensation: Evidence for self-regulation of food intake by young children. *Learning and Motivation* 16:341-355.

Birch, L. L., and M. Deysher. 1986. Caloric compensation and sensory specific satiety: Evidence for self-regulation of food intake by young children. *Appetite* 7:323-331.

Birch, L. L., and D. Marlin. 1982. I don't like it; I never tried it: Effects of exposure on two-year-old children's food preferences. *Appetite* 3:353-360.

Birch, L. L., D. Marlin and J. Rotter. 1984. Eating as the "means" activity in a contingency: Effects on young children's food preference. *Child Development* 55:532-539.

Birch, L. L., L. McPhee, D. Pirok and L. Steinberg. 1987. What kind of exposure reduces children's food neophobia? Looking versus tasting. *Appetite* 9:171-178.

Birch, L. L., L. McPhee, B. C. Shoba, L. Steinberg and R. Krehbiel. 1987. "Clean up your plate": Effects of child feeding practices on the development of intake regulation. *Learning and Motivation* 18:301-317.

Birch, L. L., S. Zimmerman and H. Hind. 1980. The influence of social affective context on preschool children's food preferences. *Child Development* 51:856-861.

Butters, J., and T. Cash. 1987. Cognitive-behavioral treatment of women's body-image dissatisfaction. *Journal of Consulting and Clinical Psychology* 55:889-897.

Capaldi, E. D., and T. L. Powley. 1990. *Taste, experience and feeding.* Washington DC: American Psychological Association.

Cash, T. F., and T. A. Brown. 1989. Gender and body images: Stereotypes and realities. *Sex Roles* 21:357-369.

Cash, T. F., and K. L. Hicks. 1990. Being fat versus thinking fat: Relationships with body image, eating behaviors, and well-being. *Cognitive Therapy and Research* 14:327-341.

Cash, T. F., and T. Pruzinsky, eds. 1990. *Body images: Development, deviance and change.* New York: Guilford Press.

Cash, T. F., B. A. Winstead and L. H. Janda. 1986. The great American shape-up: Body image survey report. *Psychology Today* 20(4): 30-37.

Collins, M. E. 1991. Promoting healthy body image through the comprehensive school health program. *Journal of Health Education* 22 (5): 297-302.

Davies, E., and A. Furnham. 1986. The dieting and body shape concerns of adolescent females. *Journal of Child Psychology and Psychiatry* 27:417-428.

Fisher, S. 1986. *Development and structure of the body image.* Hillsdale, NJ: Erlbaum.

Garner, D. M., P. E. Garfinkel, D. Schwartz and M. Thompson. 1980. Cultural expectations of thinness in women. *Psychological Reports* 47:483-491.

Giarratano, S. 1991. *Entering adulthood: Looking at body image and eating disorders.* Santa Cruz, CA: ETR Associates.

Hatfield, E., and S. Sprecher. 1988. *Mirror, mirror: The importance of looks in everyday life.* New York: SUNY Press.

Hubbard, B. M. 1991. *Entering adulthood: Moving into fitness.* Santa Cruz, CA: ETR Associates.

Hutchinson, M. G. 1985. *Transforming body image.* Trumansburg, NY: The Crossing Press.

Kenrick, D. T., and S. E. Guiterres. 1980. Contrast effects and judgments of physical attractiveness: When beauty becomes a social problem. *Journal of Personality and Social Psychology* 38:131-140.

Lacey, J. H., and S. A. Birtchnell. 1986. Body image and its disturbances. *Journal of Psychosomatic Research* 30:623-631.

Laing, S. J. 1991. *Into adolescence: A menu for good health.* Santa Cruz, CA: ETR Associates.

Matiella, A. C. 1991. *Positively different: Creating a bias-free environment for young children.* Santa Cruz, CA: ETR Associates.

Mendler, A. N. 1990. *Smiling at yourself: Educating young children about stress and self-esteem.* Santa Cruz, CA: ETR Associates.

Nasser, M. 1988. Culture and weight consciousness. *Journal of Psychosomatic Research* 32:573-577.

Noles, S. W., T. F. Cash and B. A. Winstead. 1985. Body image, physical attractiveness, and depression. *Journal of Consulting Clinical Psychology* 53:88-94.

Peck, E. B., and H. D. Ullrich. 1988. *Children and weight: A changing perspective.* Berkeley, CA: Nutrition Communications Associates.

Rozin, P., and A. E. Fallon. 1981. The acquisition of likes and dislikes for foods. In *Criteria of food acceptance: How man chooses what he eats.* J. Schims and R. L. Hall, eds. Zurich: Forster Verlag.

Silverstein, B., B. Peterson and L. Perdue. 1986. Some correlates of the thin standard of bodily attractiveness for women. *International Journal of Eating Disorders* 5:895-905.

Thompson, J. K. 1990. *Body image disturbance: Assessment and treatment.* New York: Pergamon Press.

VanderVelde, C. 1985. Body images of one's self and of others: Developmental and clinical significance. *Journal of American Psychiatric Association* 142:527-537.

About the Authors

Joanne Ikeda, MA, RD, is a cooperative extension nutrition education specialist and lecturer in the Department of Nutritional Sciences at the University of California, Berkeley. She helped design and implement a statewide program for health professionals on prevention and intervention approaches to pediatric obesity that has served as a national model. She has conducted research on the food habits of ethnic minorities, including Hmong, Hispanic and Native American communities in California. She is a past president of the California Nutrition Council and the San Francisco Bay Area Dietetic Association.

Priscilla Naworski, MS, CHES, is the director of the California Healthy Kids Resource Center. She has been active in nutrition education and comprehensive school health programs for more than 15 years. She has published curriculum guides and reviews of materials in these fields and has presented sessions at national and state nutrition and comprehensive health conferences. She has served on the California Children and Weight Task Force, which developed a position paper and training modules for health professionals who deal with children, including children who are overweight.